JURY TRIALS OUTSIDE IN

Leveraging Psychology from Discovery to Decision

JURY TRIALS OUTSIDE IN

Leveraging Psychology from Discovery to Decision

Melissa M. Gomez, PhD

MMG Jury Consulting, LLC

NATIONAL INSTITUTE FOR TRIAL ADVOCACY

Address inquiries to:

Reprint Permission
National Institute for Trial Advocacy
1685 38th Street, Suite 200
Boulder, CO 80301-2735
Phone: (800) 225-6482
Fax: (720) 890-7069
E-mail: permissions@nita.org

Library of Congress Cataloging-in-Publication Data

Names: Gomez, Melissa M., author.
Title: Jury trials outside in : leveraging psychology from discovery to
   decision / Melissa M. Gomez, PhD, MMG Jury Consulting, LLC.
Description: Boulder, CO : National Institute for Trial Advocacy, [2016]
Identifiers: LCCN 2016007588 (print) | LCCN 2016007842 (ebook) |
   ISBN 9781601565488 | ISBN 9781601565495 ()
Subjects: LCSH: Jury—United States. | Trial practice—United States. | Persuasion
   (Psychology)
Classification: LCC KF8972 .G66 2016 (print) | LCC KF8972 (ebook) |
   DDC 347.73/752—dc23
LC record available at http://lccn.loc.gov/2016007588

ISBN 978-1-60156-548-8
eISBN 978-1-60156-549-5

Cover photograph by Julia Lehman Photography.

FBA 1548

Printed in the United States.

For my boys.

CONTENTS

Foreword

Acknowledgments

Part One: Understanding Juries

1.1	Present a Consistent Picture	1
1.2	Redefine the Meaning of "Fair"	5
1.3	Account for the Third Side of the Story	8
1.4	Question the Myth of the Evil Corporation	10
1.5	Beware the Smiling Juror	13
1.6	Apply Miller's Law	15
1.7	Unleash the Power of Mad	17
1.8	Use Sympathy with Caution	20
1.9	Distinguish the Law from Jurors' Sense of Justice	24
1.10	Consider that Common Sense Isn't Always Common	28
1.11	Use Disturbing Evidence Only When Necessary	30
1.12	Turn Your Perspective Outside In	33

Part Two: Choosing Trial Strategies

2.1	Use Opposing Counsel's Momentum to Your Advantage	37
2.2	Validate the Jury's Visceral Response	39
2.3	Calculate the Impact of Omissions on Trust	41
2.4	Keep Key Points from Getting Lost in the Middle	43
2.5	Defendants: Fight Liability	46
2.6	Plaintiffs: Look Critically at Consortium Claims	48
2.7	Defendants: Address Damages	50
2.8	Plaintiffs: Assert Punitive Damages Wisely	53
2.9	Look at Your Verdict Form—Again	56

2.10 Be Wary of Online Focus Groups 59

2.11 Transactional Attorneys: Consider the Jury 62

Part Three: Deselecting Juries

3.1 Know Your Biases 65

3.2 Think Beyond a Universal Jury Profile 70

3.3 Recognize Leaders.. 73

3.4 Ask the Questions You Need to Ask..................................... 76

3.5 Don't Believe Everything You Read on the Internet..................... 80

3.6 Know the Court 83

3.7 Use Juror Questionnaires When You Can 85

3.8 Construct Voir Dire in Context 89

3.9 Keep Track of Your Jurors.. 92

Part Four: Managing Witnesses

4.1 Make a Case that Fits Your Client...................................... 95

4.2 Set the Right Foundation for Your Witness.............................. 98

4.3 Ask the Right Questions Off the Stand................................. 101

4.4 Teach Balance in Deposition.. 103

4.5 Understand Culture and Communication Values.......................... 107

4.6 Recognize Juror Mistrust in an Unreliable Witness 111

4.7 Deal with Adverse Witnesses Strategically 115

4.8 Know the Real Power of Impeaching 119

4.9 Accept that Your Witness May Not Be Likable 123

Part Five: Maintaining the Right Case Image

5.1 Never Underestimate the Power of Just Being Nice..................... 127

5.2 Recognize the Reality of Home-Field Advantage....................... 130

5.3 Investigate Public Opinion 133

5.4 Dress to Impress—Comfortably 137

5.5 Be the Right Reflection of Your Client............................... 141

FOREWORD

I have enough frequent flyer miles to circle the globe. More than once. Over the past couple of decades, they have accumulated as I travel from city to city, state to state, trial to trial. I meet lawyers, prepare witnesses, conduct research exercises, and deselect juries. I am the jury consultant. The witness coach. The jury shrink. The alleged *reader of minds* despite my constant disclaimer that I cannot, in fact, read minds.

I have been welcomed with open arms and exclamations of "You're my Doctor Phil!" I have been peered at closely and told in no uncertain terms: "I am the trial lawyer, I don't need you and your black magic"—only to later hear from that same voice: "Don't tell my client this, but you have been extremely helpful." No black magic needed.

I have seen case strategies that were triumphs. And those that were flops. I have researched juries and how they make decisions. I have watched countless attorneys make decisions and scrutinized their rationales. I have witnessed unexpected turns of events. And turns of events that were not so unexpected.

I have polled thousands of jurors and listened to what they had to say about our strategy, our tactics. Us.

I have encountered many personalities and the reactions of those personalities to being involved in litigation. I have been a sounding board for frustration, anger, and tears because lawsuits are stressful for everyone—be it the stress jurors feel in wanting to make the "right" decision; the stress witnesses feel to communicate their perspective clearly; the stress litigants feel because the outcome will impact their lives; or the stress attorneys feel in their desire to get a good result for their client.

How did I get here? I have a background in psychology. I received my PhD from the University of Pennsylvania, where I was trained in personality development, clinical practice, the psychology of learning, and effective teaching. These subjects are inherent in every jury trial, but they often take a backseat to legal issues—if they are considered at all.

As I learned through my empirical research and experience, these subjects must be in the forefront of trial strategy and planning. They penetrate every part of a case. If you want to be successful, you must pay attention to them. That is what my life's work is about. That is what this book is about.

It isn't just about how juror psychology impacts a case. It is about how the collective psychology of *all of the people involved in a case* impacts the outcome. I help lawyers bring that psychology to the forefront. Where it belongs. I help harness the power of psychology in litigation so a case is strong. And human.

I have done this work from New York to Las Vegas to Chicago to Minneapolis to Los Angeles to Dallas to Philadelphia and hundreds of places in between. Through all the cases and all the cities and all the people and all the trials, patterns take form and themes emerge about how people react, behave, and decide.

I understand that my observations of jurors, witnesses, and attorneys are manifestations of the basic principles of psychology and decision-making used in the fields of education, advertising, marketing, politics, sociology—you name it. These are not just courtroom phenomena. They are people phenomena. We should understand them. We should know how they impact our cases.

I am a believer in taking a step back to see the big picture, especially when it is so easy to get lost in the minutiae. That is my purpose as a jury consultant, and that is my goal with this book. There are so many simple, yet critical concepts that can get lost after years of dealing with briefs and depositions and motions and mediations. This book provides a review of those concepts and a tool for applying them. This books is also a collection of cases in which they were applied well—and some in which they were applied not so well. It is a conduit that connects principles that apply to civil and criminal cases, to plaintiffs and defendants, and to medical malpractice, product liability, intellectual property, contract, aviation, trucking, and all other cases that involve human beings.

My hope is that this collection of my stories, knowledge, and advice serves as an entertaining and helpful companion to both the novice and the experienced litigator. That it is relatable to anyone who has to tell their story to a decision-maker, whether a judge, mediator, arbitrator, or juror. That it helps you, as the reader, take that step back to see your case and its people from a new perspective—by considering everyone's perspective.

ACKNOWLEDGMENTS

I am grateful.

It is in the process of doing something nutty like writing a book in which you truly recognize the support you have around you. It is an unbelievably humbling feeling.

Paula Riley read and reread my stories so many times she probably knows them better than I do. She made the prose tighter and the messages stronger. She made the book better.

Jacqui Breslin and Laura Snee helped me with hours upon hours of research and edits. They made the book come together.

Renee Lemley and Elise Zealand. I have no words for these two masters of the written word. They are true friends and strong women who know how to be support-ive and tough all at once. They helped me see this project differently and make the right organizational changes. They made the book smarter.

Jim Pabarue and Jim Gordon provided reactions to the book from the perspec-tive of the litigators it was written for. Their insights were invaluable and their time precious. They made the book more useful.

Bill Hinchman connected me to the wonderful organization, NITA, its publishing department, and LexisNexis. He was incredibly positive and supportive of the project. He gave the book a stage.

Jim Smith, Willie Simmons, Jim Brogan, Richard Walter, Gina Harris, Paul D'Amato, Kim Mandelbaum, Alan Feldman, and Larry Muscarella have supported me over the years with unwavering faith in my work. They have trusted me with their important cases—a trust I do not take lightly. It is in working with them that I have developed a passion for what I do. They, among many others, gave the book its stories.

Dan Ansa, my mentor and dear friend, refused to let me give up until I "crossed the finish line." In the loving fashion of a Marine lieutenant colonel, he gave me no other option but to see it through. Jeanne Stanley, Kristen Caldwell, and Michael Butler were incredible support in a markedly less military style as I wrote, refined, and wrote some more. They gave me belief in myself because they believed in me.

And through all of it were my guys at home who dealt with (and still deal with) my days on the road, away from home, traveling from trial to trial, collecting my stories. And they still manage to be my biggest cheerleaders. Nick, Max, and Oliver. They gave me the reason to start in the first place.

PART ONE

UNDERSTANDING JURIES

1.1   Present a Consistent Picture

There is a theory of psychology that conceptually captures my core philosophy of the jury trial. It embodies the reasons why the image you project at trial, as a whole, is so important. That theory is called Gestalt psychology. It was developed by Max Wertheimer, a scholar who, interestingly, started his career in the study of law, but later turned his interests to philosophy. In its simplest terms, Gestalt psychology looks at the human experience through Aristotle's quote "the whole is greater than the sum of its parts." Essentially, it is about the human response to the entirety of an experience. What we perceive is beyond the simple senses of seeing and hearing. Instead, we integrate all sensory experience into one meaningful whole.

What we perceive is beyond the simple senses of seeing and hearing. Instead, we integrate all sensory experience into one meaningful whole.

In Gestalt psychology theory, human beings are predisposed to search for a whole and a meaning. Not just in what one sees and hears, but also in what one perceives. This is about how we organize information in a way that makes sense in our minds.

An example of a Gestalt is listening to a piece of music. When listening to a song, we do not hear a collection of separate instruments, vocal sounds, or notes. We perceive one continuous tune: one meaningful experience of a song. We may also think of a string of holiday lights that blink in sequence. As opposed to seeing a series of separate lights turning on and off, we observe the movement of light traveling around a Christmas tree or over the silhouette of a house. So experiencing a Gestalt is perceiving a collection of stimuli and incorporating that collection into one whole experience with meaning separate from that of each individual stimulus.

An effective story in a trial should work like that collection of notes, that song we hear as a meaningful melody—as one integrated experience to which we tap our toes and sing along. The pieces must fit together in a way that presents a whole picture. Consistently.

I remember a case that perfectly illustrated how Gestalt psychology is at play in the courtroom: as the completion of a trial involving a contract dispute between two companies in Los Angeles neared, I was working on closing arguments with the lead attorney. We were representing the plaintiff, which was the larger organization in the case. The defendants were a smaller company and its president. At one point during our work on the closing, the lead attorney asked me, "What do you think is the biggest strength of our case?" I thought for a moment, looked up, and said one word: "Consistency."

What I meant, and what I explained in response to the puzzled expression I received, was something that applies to every trial everywhere. I have yet to find an exception.

By saying "consistency," I meant the consistency of overall image. It was about the way the pieces of the trial came together comprehensively. It wasn't only about the evidence that supported our arguments, but also about the peripheral messages sent through the behaviors, demeanor, and tactics of both sides of the courtroom. These messages created a Gestalt that encapsulated our story.

In this case, the defendants accused our client of being sloppy, underhanded, and disorganized in its business practice. They accused the business of being run by a selfish person who cared not for the company, but only for his own personal gain. In response, we presented the image of our client as a well-oiled machine. While the business culture may not be warm and fuzzy, we argued that the business was run honestly and with integrity. It was a business and a good one. We championed a position that, in fact, the defendants were the sneaky and underhanded ones, syphoning money from our client's company as if it were the defendants' personal ATM.

Image was particularly important considering the accusations each side made about the other. We knew that if the jurors were to perceive our client as professional and competent, we needed not only to argue that image on behalf of the client, but we, the legal team, had to embody it ourselves through words and actions. We had to become the Gestalt we wanted to project. All of the instruments of our case had to work together so the jurors could hear the melody of our song. And hopefully, they would sing along.

The strategy to project our desired image took form as early as voir dire. Specifically, during jury selection, opposing counsel questioned jurors for an inordinate amount of time. They tried to ingratiate themselves with questions that had nothing to do with the case facts—asking about bumper stickers, favorite sports teams, magazines, television shows . . . the list went on. Don't get me wrong, these kinds of rapport-building questions can lighten the atmosphere of the courtroom and give you good information about a person and his or her values. But they can backfire if overused. And, they were well overused. Too much was too much.

Opposing counsel appeared unprepared. The attorney conducting voir dire seemed to be making up the questions as he went along and lacked a discernable structure to his process. Regardless of whether it was true, it certainly looked as though he had not reviewed the extensive questionnaires the jurors had filled out several days before. Of course, the behavior of the opposition was nothing we could control, but we were thankful for it regardless.

(*We hear the beat of the percussion.*)

When it was our turn, we consciously acted like the well-run, no-nonsense business model that we wanted the jurors to associate with our client. Counsel was polite and organized. It was obvious that we were prepared and had spent time reviewing the juror questionnaire forms. We were ready with our follow-up on the questionnaire information the jurors had provided, and the extensive markings we put on the forms were apparent as we referred to them. The few questions counsel asked were directly relevant.

Can you start to see how the images of the parties were beginning to form?

(*Other instruments join in harmony.*)

Image messages continued throughout the trial. The other side treated the courtroom like its personal domain. There was an entourage of young, beautiful women at counsel table beside the defendant. Visitors came in and out of the courtroom noisily, distracting attention from the process. There was obvious fumbling with documents and sneaky trial tactics that were revealed in front of the jury and, thus, backfired. We could not have asked for a better picture of the defendants if we had been able to dictate it ourselves.

(*Cue the lyrics.*)

In light of what was happening with the opposition in the courtroom, we took the opportunity to highlight even more strongly our "business is business" approach by acting in stark contrast. As in voir dire, we made sure documents were readily available on a moment's notice. Each person who entered into our side of the courtroom was briefed on what to wear and how to behave—not only in, but anywhere near the courthouse. We were on time, concise, and thorough. We were respectful of the rules of the courtroom just like we claimed our client was respectful of the rules of business and contracts. We made sure every one of our witnesses knew about and reflected this image.

(*And the melody is heard.*)

In the end, like the arrangement of musical instruments that create the perception of one song, the pieces of the trial came together for each side to develop a big picture of the parties that told the story for the jurors even without the content of the evidence. The plaintiff won, in part, because both the plaintiffs' and defendants' case images were consistent with the story the plaintiff wanted to tell. The Gestalt that we championed at trial was effectively personified. By both sides. It was not just the evidence. It was the total picture.

The point is this: Trial is more than just law and evidence. As a jury consultant, I believe it is imperative to examine all of the pieces of a case and how they come together. It is vital to evaluate how the peripheral messages support or refute your positions.

Just as important, be cognizant of the image messages you relay about the other side of the case and whether it is likely that the peripheral messages jurors will see in the courtroom reflect or contradict that image. In the above contract case, we were lucky that the defendants gave us the gift of their poor behavior, thereby bringing our accusations to life for the jurors to see firsthand. Such strong image-related accusations can backfire if the opposition presents itself in stark contrast to the image you paint of their client. If jurors don't see what you claim in either the evidence or the image of the opposition, it is your image that will suffer. The melody becomes cacophony.

Questions to Ask Yourself

- What is the overall image I want presented of my case/client?
- How is that desired image reflected in each element of my case?
- Is that desired image contradicted by any element of my case?
- What is the overall image I am presenting of the opposition?
- How will my desired image of the opposition likely be reflected or contradicted by the elements of the opposition's case?

1.2 Redefine the Meaning of "Fair"

In my career as a jury consultant, I have been repeatedly confronted with the concept of what it means to have a fair trial. For example, the criminal child molestation trial of Jerry Sandusky made national headlines in 2012. I received calls from several newspapers and news stations to provide commentary from a jury perspective. The courthouse sat in the shadow of Penn State University, for whom Mr. Sandusky was the former assistant football coach. Each reporter asked about the implications of jurors' connections with the University and, considering those connections, if it was possible for Jerry Sandusky to get a fair trial? It raised a question that I have pondered often over my years working with juries: what does it mean for any trial to be "fair?"

Anaïs Nin wisely wrote, "We don't see things as they are, we see things as we are." So if we consider the concept of fair as having jurors who come to trial as blank slates upon whom the trial evidence is placed and weighed, then no one can have a fair trial. Ever. It is just not the way human minds work. Instead, it is human nature that people will view any case through the spectacles of their own unique experience. Individually. Idiosyncratically.

So if we consider the concept of fair as having jurors who come to trial as blank slates upon whom the trial evidence is placed and weighed, then no one can have a fair trial.

Looking to the fields of art and literature, individual and diverse interpretations of meaning have been both celebrated and debated. Paul Armstrong (1983) discusses how intellectual perspectives on meaning in literature conflict, as some theorists "insist that any literary work has a single, determinate meaning and others argue that there are no limits to the reading a text allows."[1] So in the literary context, regardless of whether there *should* be one or more than one "truth" in the meaning, the fact of the matter is different minds do interpret literary and artistic works differently. That is the way that human minds work.

Our minds process information no differently whether looking at a Rembrandt, reading J. D. Salinger's *Catcher in the Rye,* interpreting meaning in day-to-day communication, or analyzing the facts in a jury trial. Although jurors are certainly not expected to look at a trial to form an artistic interpretation, they are certainly asked to deduce meaning. So we should not be surprised that, as in literature and art, meanings gleaned from a case story can vary wildly based on the mind developing that meaning, regardless of whether there *should* be only one meaning, or one truth, to be construed.

---

1. Paul B. Armstrong, *The Conflict of Interpretations and the Limits of Pluralism*, 98 MODERN LANGUAGE ASSOCIATION 341 (1983).

A juror's experience with or opinion about the relevant subject matter will certainly give that person a perspective before hearing case facts, but does this mean that person can't be fair? The answer resides in the relevance of that experience to the person, the strength of opinion, and how that opinion comports with the evidence provided at trial.

There is a theory regarding the psychology of learning known as *proactive interference* theory. This theory relates to a phenomenon in which either memories or the way we have previously learned to behave and think can impede our comprehension of new material. Simple studies of proactive interference have shown reduction in how people retain and recall word lists[2] and single words[3] after the passage of time and under the influence of a prior task.

By taking these simple studies and relating them in the larger context of how the human brain learns, psychologists understand that proactive interference occurs in any given context, including the courtroom, where past learning is salient enough to inhibit a person's full potential to retain case information that is inconsistent with that past learning.

Therefore, the question isn't about whether people *have* experience. They do. The question also isn't whether we can erase that experience from their minds. We can't. Instead, it comes down to whether the experience outside the courtroom will take priority over the evidence or will the evidence take priority over the experience? In other words, it is not just the experience in and of itself that is relevant. It is the strength of that prior learning and the extent to which it is likely to impede that juror's ability or willingness to learn, understand, and retain the evidence as it is presented at trial.

You can't eliminate preconceived opinions in your jury pool completely, no matter how good you think you are at jury selection. Instead, you can hope to use the voir dire process to identify and remove people whose prior learning method closes their minds to your story. What you have left are people who still may be skeptical. Is this fair? I can't say that it is or is not, but it is the system we have. Keep in mind that in any given trial, this issue affects both sides. Admittedly, though, it often can be more troubling to one side over the other, depending on the case and the venue.

You must make sure that your strategy accounts for the people who are hearing it. Don't expect them to change their perspectives for you and your case. They won't.

---

2. Leo Postman & Geoffrey Keppel, *Conditions of Cumulative Proactive Inhibition*, 106 JOURNAL OF EXPERIMENTAL PSYCHOLOGY 376 (1977).
3. Geoffrey Keppel & B. J. Underwood, *Proactive Inhibition in Short-Term Retention of Single Items*, 1 JOURNAL OF VERBAL LEARNING AND VERBAL BEHAVIOR 153 (1962).

As a result, it is imperative that you understand, as much as possible, the mindset of the jurors and their community before you go to trial so you can tell a story that accounts for that mindset. If your arguments are contrary to a widely held belief, proactive interference will block your message and you will be unlikely to succeed. You must make sure that your strategy accounts for the people who are hearing it. Don't expect them to change their perspectives for you and your case. They won't.

So, let's go back to Mr. Sandusky. Did a connection with Penn State automatically render jurors incapable of being fair and impartial? The judge didn't think so, and as I told reporters and their news cameras, neither did I. The issue was whether a juror, given her background and experience, regardless of connections to the Penn State community, was willing to listen to both sides and consider the evidence. The jurors in the trial took two days to deliberate, requesting some of the testimony to be read back to them. To me, that seems to pass for careful consideration of the evidence. As for the verdict, you can decide for yourself whether a couple hundred years behind bars was a fair and just result.

Questions to Ask Yourself

- What juror experiences/perceptions will affect the way a juror sees my case?

- Is the strength of a particular juror's experience/perception such that it will likely close that juror's mind to my case arguments?

- Are there any relevant community events, values, or characteristics of my trial venue that may have a direct impact on perceptions of my case?

- Are my case arguments congruent with or contradictory toward jurors' likely experiences and perceptions?

1.3   Account for the Third Side of the Story

There are aspects of the way jury trials are held that are simply inconsistent with the way people make decisions, not the least of which is the court's request that jurors only use the evidence provided in the courtroom as the basis of their decisions. Even assuming that everyone follows the instruction not to perform their own Internet searches, sitting back and passively receiving information is simply not the way that people operate.

In a mock trial I conducted about a business dispute, there was a moment in which I was introducing the defense presentation after the participants had heard that of the plaintiffs. During that introduction, I said, "As we all know, there are two sides to every story." One of the panel members quickly retorted, "There are actually three: what this side says, what that side says, and what actually happened."

People are information seekers. They are active learners. How often are we instructed not to blindly accept what we are told or what we read? Consequently, jurors at trial like to become their own sleuths. They believe that both sides have an agenda and the truth likely lies somewhere in between—somewhere outside of what they are being told.

Consequently, jurors at trial like to become their own sleuths. They believe that both sides have an agenda and the truth likely lies somewhere in between—somewhere outside of what they are being told.

Take the case of an OB-GYN in Chicago accused of telling a patient it was safe to become pregnant too soon after a rupture of her uterine wall. The wall ruptured again during the delivery of the child, and the baby died. For this trial, the defense team employed a shadow jury, who watched the proceedings as the real jurors did and without knowing which side of the case had hired them. The shadow jurors provided us daily feedback on what they observed during the course of the trial.

During openings, as the plaintiff's attorney addressed the jury, explaining the allegations against the defendant, the doctor would visibly squirm at counsel table. He twisted his arms and legs into what looked like a crazy yoga pose. In the first few hours of trial, the shadow jurors began to call the defendant "Pretzel Man." In the interviews I conducted with them during the first break of the day, the jurors stated that they found it helpful to watch Pretzel Man because, as they explained, when he "pretzeled," that meant it was time to pay attention. Something important must be happening. Why else would he get so visibly upset? I quickly removed myself from the shadow jurors to make the necessary phone calls that would ensure that such pretzeling ceased immediately.

It is the perspective of a truth that exists outside of what they are being told that leads jurors to look beyond the case presented to them to find information that will lead to that third side of the story. Sometimes that information isn't even found inside the courtroom.

In a small county in the Midwest, the plaintiff was seeking millions of dollars for a personal injury, claiming that the defendant's negligence had rendered him incapable of working in his technology consulting profession. Every day of the trial, this plaintiff went to an eatery during the lunch break and clicked away at his computer. Some jurors observed this. It certainly looked like he was working to them. Verdict for the defense.

During trial, you and your client are being scrutinized—and not just in the courtroom. Do you wait for the light before you cross the street? Who are you talking to in the hall? Did you hold the elevator for someone or let it close in their face? These are just some of the key peripheral cues jurors-turned-sleuths collect to find that third side of the story: the story that includes who you really are and who your client really is. This is the side of the story that they will call the "truth."

Questions to Ask Yourself

- What peripheral information exists in the courtroom that may become "evidence" to the jurors?

- What peripheral information exists outside of and around the courtroom that may become "evidence" to the jurors?

- How am I keeping tabs on and controlling that peripheral information so it does not negatively impact my case?

1.4 Question the Myth of the Evil Corporation

I have repeatedly encountered a belief among attorneys that, in my experience, has typically been established to be untrue. What is the belief? Jurors hate companies just for being companies. Jurors believe profit-seeking is evil. No exceptions.

It's no wonder people think that there is such a pervasive anti-corporate bias in the United States given high-profile movements such as Occupy Wall Street that began in New York City as a reaction to the 2007 economic crisis. The movement, in essence, declared a media war against corporations and the wealthy "one percent." The movement proudly touts on its website, "We kick the ass of the ruling class."

The entertainment industry also often presents corporations in a negative light. Just look at the popularity of Michael Moore and his films, including *Roger & Me*, *Sicko*, and *Capitalism: A Love Story*. In these films, Moore takes on the automotive and pharmaceutical industries and fights against corporate interests pursuing profit over public good. In the John Grisham novel, *The Rainmaker*, a young lawyer takes on an insurance company after that company refused to pay for treatment that could have saved a sick young man's life. In the film version of the courtroom drama, the man's mother reads a letter she received from the insurance company after multiple requests for the treatment to be funded. In the letter she read aloud to the jurors, the insurance company, once again, denied coverage and wrote, "you must be stupid, stupid, stupid" for continuing her repeated pleas for help. We may also consider the stories portrayed in *Wall Street*, *The Wolf of Wall Street*, *Bonfire of the Vanities*, and *A Civil Action*—the list of films that portray the lack of ethics in business and the manner in which people lose their moral foundation for the gain of the almighty dollar goes on.

It should go without saying that jurors' visceral and ingrained perception is that corporations are immoral and act in disregard for the good of people. The thing is, in my experience, I have not found that to be the case.

Anti-corporate sentiments are certainly not modern phenomena. Historical figures have made strong statements about big business going back hundreds of years. Seventeenth-century English philosopher Thomas Hobbes called corporations "worms in the body politic." William Gouge in his 1833 publication *A Short History of Paper Money and Banking in the United States* wrote: "Against corporations of every kind, the objection may be brought that whatever power is given to them is so much taken from either the government or the people."[4] In *The Devil's Dictionary*,

---

4. WILLIAM GOUGE, A SHORT HISTORY OF PAPER MONEY AND BANKING IN THE UNITED STATES (printed by TW Ustick and for sale by Grigg & Elliott, Uriah Hunt and Hogan & Thompson. Reprinted in 1968 by Augustus M. Kelley Publishers) (1833).

published in 1911, Ambrose Bierce defined a corporation as "an ingenious device for obtaining individual profit without individual responsibility."[5]

So, considering the historical pervasiveness of anti-corporate perceptions, it should go without saying that jurors' visceral and ingrained perception is that corporations are immoral and act in disregard for the good of people. The thing is, in my experience, I have not found that to be the case.

What I have seen instead is that most reasonable people understand that the nature of business is making money. Profitability makes companies successful. It creates jobs. It is good for our society. It is the American way. The net effect is that most jurors do not automatically believe that a company is corrupt just because it's a company, but they do want to understand how a particular company behaved in a way that is either consistent with, or deviates from, expectations of how companies *normally* behave.

Don't get me wrong, there certainly are people who will mistrust anything a company does. These people, though, don't appear to be in the majority. Through data I have collected nationally from about 400 jury-eligible adults, 82 percent disagreed that they would automatically give an individual the benefit of the doubt over a company in a lawsuit. In an additional sample I collected from 390 jury-eligible adults, over half (54 percent) rejected the notion that most corporations are more interested in profits than safety.

So what does this all mean for a jury trial? Well, there are several implications that can be described through mistakes I have seen made by plaintiffs and defendants alike. First, I have seen plaintiffs' counsel provide presentations to juries about evil corporations and "profits over people" in cases in which there was simply no indication that the company had any ill intent, regardless of whether it made a mistake or not.

Overstating the "evil" of an organization tends to have a negative effect for plaintiffs. In essence, the plaintiff raises the bar for what she has to prove. It takes a lot more evidence to prove that a company is an evil organization with a devious plot to hide its wrongdoings than to tell a story of a company that made an error that caused the plaintiff harm. I have often seen jurors argue in focus groups that "business is business" and that "Company X never meant for this to happen." When the plaintiff has made the argument that Company X purposely ignored safety to make more profit, "purposely" becomes what jurors want proved—not because that is what the law says, but because that is what the plaintiff said.

On the corporate defense side, I have seen defense attorneys, fearing anti-corporate bias, try to deny that their corporate clients' primary concern is profits. I remember a securities case in which investors in a multi-billion dollar company sued that company for a loss in their investment value after a government investigation. In this case, the

---

5. AMBROSE BIERCE, THE DEVIL'S DICTIONARY (first published in book form as THE CYNIC'S WORD-BOOK, 1906) (Neale Publishing Co. 1911).

defense counsel wanted the founder and CEO of the multi-billion dollar enterprise to tell the jury that he founded the business, which supplied materials to the government, for purely altruistic purposes—to provide a helpful service to his country. Well, that may have been part of it, but no one will believe that this businessman decided to get into such a lucrative business without the goal of making a profit, especially considering that the business made him extremely wealthy. Businesspeople like profit. Trying to convince jurors of anything different doesn't seem honest. Because it isn't.

In that case, instead of running away from the company's profitability (which appeared to jurors as an admission that there was something wrong with the manner profitability was attained), we got a better response by embracing the company's profitability. Good business is profitable. That is part of what makes it good business.

Most people don't expect companies to have a high level of morality.
They are, however, supposed to have integrity.

The point is that both sides need to make arguments congruent with juror perceptions, keeping in mind that these perceptions are not overwhelmingly negative toward companies, but they do contain high expectations. For example, in a sample of 1,340 jury-eligible adults, 69 percent believed that in a lawsuit, what a company is obligated to do legally is more important to consider than what it should have done morally. Legal obligation, as long as no underlying ill-intent becomes apparent, is where most jurors focus. Most people don't expect companies to have a high level of morality. They are, however, supposed to have integrity.

For the plaintiff, attacking a company for no other reason than the fact that it is a company is unlikely to fly. There has to be something specific about the company's actions that deviate from what people perceive as normal corporate behavior. For the defense, there is no reason to run away from the corporate image. In fact, I see defendants do better when they embrace the corporate image and introduce evidence that the company knows its business and runs that business well.

Questions to Ask Yourself

- What are the likely expectations jurors will have of the corporation in my case?

- How are jurors' likely expectations met or not met in the story of my case?

- Does the evidence in my case reflect corporate malfeasance?

- Am I presenting the intentions of the corporation in a manner that will affect my credibility or burden in the eyes of the jurors?

1.5 Beware the Smiling Juror

I have been asked on more than one occasion to observe jurors in court and provide analyses of their body language. It begs the question of whether one can tell what someone is feeling, thinking, or who he favors based on his body language in the courtroom? The simple answer is: "No, you can't."

For that reason, when I am in court, I direct my attention to the detail of the proceedings, the credibility of the witnesses, and the messages that are being relayed on each side. Do I keep an eye on the jurors? Of course. Am I trying to read their body language to discover what they are thinking? No.

The most commonly cited statistic puts the level of interpersonal communication considered to be "nonverbal" at 93 percent. As a result, it is a natural inclination to want to tap into the manner jurors communicate with us nonverbally in the courtroom. After all, we are not permitted to exchange words or ask them what they think about our case. All we have is what we can see.

Do I keep an eye on the jurors? Of course. Am I trying to read their body language to discover what they are thinking? No.

The problem is, however, that nonverbal cues have multiple meanings. Thus, in most instances, we cannot determine which meaning is being communicated by a particular nonverbal cue at a particular time. For example, a nod can mean agreement, understanding, or just that a person is listening. Of course, we also have the ever-mysterious "smiling juror." Many of us may have encountered that person who looks right at us when we give our presentations with a grin on her face. This person can make us feel good because a smile is typically a friendly gesture by someone who likes us and agrees with us . . . unless it is not. That beaming smile can also be a sign that this particular juror is happy to have the opportunity to stick it to us the first chance she gets.

Dr. Albert Mehrabian, a scholar whose work has focused on nonverbal communication, conducted several studies on the subject. As explained in his book, *Silent Messages*,[6] Mehrabian studied all of the different aspects of nonverbal communication, including body positions, movements, and facial expressions.

Through his work, Mehrabian illustrated how that 93 percent statistic is explained. He found that 7 percent of any message is conveyed through words, 38 percent through vocal elements, and 55 percent through completely nonverbal elements (facial expressions, gestures, posture, etc.). Subtracting the 7 percent for actual substantive content from 100 percent of total communication leaves us with 93 percent.

---

6. ALBERT MEHRABIAN, SILENT MESSAGES: IMPLICIT COMMUNICATION OF EMOTIONS AND ATTITUDES (1981).

Nonverbal communication is not just body language, but all aspects of communication working together. Correctly interpreting one piece of communication outside the context of the other pieces can be difficult, if not impossible. You can get a sense of general emotion, but not the thinking behind it. Full understanding of communication is experienced alongside other cues such as verbal tone and content. In the context of juries, you are interpreting nonverbal communications without any other contextual cue and that can lead you to misinterpret the intention.

One piece of information I do get from nonverbal behavior is whether or not jurors are paying attention. Their eyes are open, their gaze moves along with where the action is happening in the courtroom, and they may be leaning forward. That said, we can't always be certain that a person is *not* paying attention. There are people who are auditory learners and shut their eyes to listen more intently. More than once I have observed mock trial jurors who appeared to sleep through the presentations, but then recite detailed facts in deliberation. They weren't sleeping. They were shutting down their other senses to listen more intently. As far as those jurors who are actively paying attention are concerned, can I tell whether they are paying attention because they like our case or don't like our case? Not typically, but at least we know we are keeping them awake. That's a start.

Essentially, the task of trying to read the meaning of nonverbal behaviors can be fruitless and tiring, and there is really not much you can do except continue to present your case. Unless, of course, the jurors are actually asleep—complete with head nodding, drooling, or snoring (yes, I have seen it happen in both mock and real trials). Those are typically nonverbal behaviors whose meaning we can all understand.

Questions to Ask Yourself

- What nonverbal communication am I receiving from the jurors?
- Can I really interpret what that communication means?
- Are my jurors staying awake?
- What can I do to keep my jurors awake and engaged?

1.6 Apply Miller's Law

In case you were wondering, there is a reason why phone numbers have seven digits. It is because studies in human learning have found that most people can only retain up to seven pieces of new information at once. After the number of pieces of new information cross the magic number seven, they start to get lost in our minds. It is just too much for most people to retain in their short-term memory, which is that place in our brains where we actively hold new pieces of information.

In 1956, Princeton University scholar George A. Miller published one of the most frequently referenced papers in the field of psychology: "The Magical Number Seven, Plus or Minus Two: Some Limits on Our Capacity for Processing Information."[7] This paper reported that the number of objects an average human can hold in working memory is about seven, give or take a couple. This phenomenon even has a name. It's called Miller's Law.

Miller's Law has been studied in several different ways. Researchers have used verbal presentations of lists of numbers and words and found that people remember up to about seven items before memory starts to drop other items out. The rule of seven has also been studied visually by showing research participants quick glimpses of pictures with a number of dots or other shapes and then asking them to report how many shapes they saw. Again, folks tend to perceive the number of items accurately until about seven, and then they need to guess or estimate when larger numbers are presented.

Considering that people tend to remember only about seven pieces of new information at a time, it is critical to evaluate how much information we are asking jurors to remember at trial.

When I conduct mock trials, I engage the surrogate jurors in focus sessions after the exercise to get a clear understanding of how they perceived the case. I ask why they made the decisions they made, what stood out as strong evidence for one side or another, and to what they paid the most attention. Regardless of the complexity of the case, jurors reliably will focus on a few main arguments or pieces of information. Usually no more than six or . . . seven.

It is critical to take control of the information jurors will retain by narrowing your focus to your strongest evidence and key messages.

A mock trial is typically held in one day with truncated evidence. Jurors will have more time to digest information during a real trial, moving repeated information from short- to long-term memory, which has more storage space. Therefore, I am

---

7. George A. Miller, *The Magical Number Seven, Plus or Minus Two: Some Limits on Our Capacity for Processing Information*, 63 Psychological Review 81 (1956).

not saying that you could, or should, whittle a complex commercial case down to seven pieces of evidence.

Instead, what I am saying is that you should simplify a case to no more than seven overarching concepts (and the fewer the better) into which you can clearly categorize evidence. This way, even though jurors will not remember every piece of evidence, they will be able to keep straight in their minds the subset of key points into which they can organize the more detailed pieces of evidence. As long as the jurors retain the overarching points, losing the specifics within them is less of a problem.

If you throw too much information at jurors, they will remember only some of that information. Different jurors will remember different pieces. You won't get to choose what is collectively remembered and what is lost. It is critical to take control of the information jurors will retain by narrowing your focus to your strongest evidence and key messages. The number of pieces of evidence in most trials will obviously go beyond the magic number seven, but keep Miller's Law in mind as you make decisions about trial strategy. Present key points and decide what you will emphasize in openings and closings.

Evidence is only helpful at trial when your decision-makers remember it.

The critical point is this: Evidence is only helpful at trial when your decision-makers remember it.

Questions to Ask Yourself

- What are the key, overarching messages I want the jury to understand and remember?

- How can I organize my case so that the evidence fits into these overarching points?

- How many points am I trying to make?

- Am I asking the jurors to remember too much?

- Where can or should I scale back to make it easier for my jurors?

1.7   Unleash the Power of Mad

Sympathy is a central part of many jury trials, but, from what I have found in my experience, the true jury award accelerator is anger.

In general, jurors tend to look at money damages in two ways: what the plaintiff deserves to receive and what the defendant deserves to pay. When looking simply at what a plaintiff deserves to receive, sympathy plays a role, but so do other factors. Jurors often are critical of, and naturally curious about, the plaintiff's own role in what happened to him and the extent to which he has done what he needs to do to mitigate his damages.

In general, jurors tend to look at money damages in two ways: what the plaintiff deserves to receive and what the defendant deserves to pay.

When evaluating what a plaintiff deserves to receive in damages, the jury may question why this plaintiff deserves millions of dollars for injuries when the jurors themselves may have experienced their own injuries (or those of loved ones) and have neither received, nor asked for, a dime.

I recall a plaintiff in a small Pennsylvania town who fell several stories while working on a tall structure after his fall protection equipment failed. While the jurors accepted that the equipment did, in fact, fail, they were critical that the plaintiff did not have his back-up fall protection connected. During the mock trial deliberations, they argued that despite the failure of the equipment, if he had fulfilled his obligations toward his own safety, he would have been left dangling in the air attached to his secondary fall protection instead of falling all the way to the ground. The jurors deemed the failed equipment defective, but strongly reduced the damages because of what they perceived as the plaintiff's own failure.

When dealing with what a defendant deserves to pay, however, jurors who find behavior blatant or egregious or who find a defendant arrogant or dismissive of the plaintiff and her injuries will often make that defendant pay through the nose despite what they believe a plaintiff deserves. This is true regardless of whether there is a line on the verdict sheet for punitive damages.

Jennifer Lerner of Carnegie Mellon University and Larissa Tiedens of Stanford University (2006) studied the impact of anger on judgment and decision-making. In their article, "Portrait of the Angry Decision Maker: How Appraisal Tendencies Shape Anger's Influence on Cognition," they write, "Once activated, anger can color people's perceptions, form their decisions, and guide their behavior, regardless of whether the decisions at hand have anything to do with the source of one's anger."[8]

---

8. Jennifer S. Lerner & Larissa Z. Tiedens, *Portrait of the Angry Decision Maker: How Appraisal Tendencies Shape Anger's Influence on Cognition,* 19 JOURNAL OF BEHAVIORAL DECISION MAKING 115 (2006).

In their review of the documented study and observations of the mechanisms behind anger, they found that anger causes people to process information more eagerly and less thoughtfully than a person who is not angry. Anger inhibits objectivity and rationality. Interestingly, as compared to other emotions, angry people having higher confidence that their judgment is correct or justified. Therefore, judgment is less carefully self-scrutinized.[9]

It is important to note that there is more work involved in managing juror anger than sympathy at trial. Sympathy is natural and automatic. It tends to hit immediately, and jurors marinate in it throughout trial. It also tends to fade as jurors become used to the idea of what happened. They get desensitized. Anger, on the other hand, grows.

There is more work involved in managing juror anger than sympathy at trial. Sympathy is natural and automatic. It tends to hit immediately, and jurors marinate in it throughout trial. It also tends to fade as jurors become used to the idea of what happened. They get desensitized. Anger, on the other hand, grows.

In a Philadelphia case in which a child was killed in an appliance fire, jurors struggled with what the child's mother deserved in compensation. The death was tragic, and the natural sympathy toward this mother, watching and hearing her child perish in the way she did, was automatic and strong. There was evidence, though, that this mother had left the child in the room with the burning appliance to get some water, only to find the child trapped by the fire in that room when she returned. Jurors struggled with rewarding a mother in the death of a child for whom she had a clear opportunity to get out of harm's way. In the mock trial, this debate was heated among the jurors. I was working for the plaintiff, and this debate caused us great concern.

During the actual trial, as the case was presented against the defendant manufacturer, the evidence was compelling that the company knew that this appliance caused other fatal fires. When the corporate witnesses were on the stand, the jurors perceived the witnesses as arrogant and unlikable and unable to answer questions about what the company did with that knowledge. The witnesses also admitted that the company destroyed the evidence from those prior fatal fires after its own investigations had concluded.

For the pièce de résistance of the trial, the defense pointed to an unidentified object in a photograph as the alternative cause of the fire. Unfortunately for the defense, that object turned out to be a bag that was found, brought to the courtroom, and waved in the air for the jurors during plaintiff's closing.

---

9. *Id.*

By the time they went into deliberations, the jurors were angry. Very angry. Not only were they angered by the lack of corporate action in response to knowledge of its product's known history of fires, but this perceived "bad" behavior was further illustrated by what was seen as "bad" behavior in the courtroom. Specifically, the jurors found that the defense presented misleading arguments and unlikable corporate representatives. In deliberations, anger pervaded the decision-making. The mother's failings no longer mattered, and the damage award made headlines.

Questions to Ask Yourself

- Is this case solely about sympathy, or does anger have a part in it?
- Where will jurors criticize both the defendant's and the plaintiff's story of the case?
- What about my case is likely to make jurors angry?
- How will that anger benefit or hurt my case?
- What can I do to increase or mitigate that anger to my case's benefit?

1.8 Use Sympathy with Caution

In research on the influence of sympathy in criminal jury trials, Bryan Meyers and Edith Greene (2004) studied the effect of victim impact statements in the sentencing phase in capital punishment case. Victim impact statements are written or oral statements made by a crime victim or the surviving family members of a deceased victim about the harm they suffered as the result of the crime. It is no surprise that Meyers and Greene found that these statements caused jurors to be more punitive toward the defendant.[10]

With the intuitive understanding of the impact of sympathy on juror emotions and, thus, decisions, I have seen plaintiffs in civil trials find it difficult to resist a strong push on the emotional story of the case. At first blush, it makes sense to try and elicit an increased punitive mindset against a defendant even if punitive damages are not available in the case.

However, Meyers and Greene express their concern about the sympathetic nature of victim impact statements. They question whether the statements cause jurors to make emotional sentencing decisions on the *result* of the crime instead of the *nature and context* of the actual crime. They question whether the emotion elicited by the impact statements is detrimental to the process by improperly affecting decision-makers through information that is not legally relevant.[11]

Considering the manner in which I see plaintiffs push the emotional story of their cases, it makes me wonder if the same issue comes to bear in jurors' minds when it is *they* who feel that the plaintiff is over-emphasizing the emotion and ignoring the nature of the liability claims, especially given jurors' knowledge that the end game of a civil trial is money.

Sympathy is a natural and powerful emotion. The problem is that when sympathy is overplayed, jurors feel manipulated. When people feel emotionally manipulated, they become angry toward the perceived manipulator.

What can happen when jurors perceive that sympathy has been overplayed? I remember one such case involving the tragic death of a child in a power-equipment accident.

For the first two days of trial, plaintiff's counsel put family member after family member on the stand, talking about the horrendous accident and its impact on the child's family. By the end of those two days, everyone in the courtroom, including

---

10. Bryan Myers & Edith Greene, *The Prejudicial Nature of Victim Impact Statements: Implications for Capital Sentencing Policy*, 10 Psychology, Public Policy and Law 492 (2004).
11. *Id.*

myself and especially the jurors, were emotionally drained. The problem for the plaintiff, though, was that no one yet understood why this unthinkable tragedy was the defendant's fault. Testimony about the alleged failings of the equipment came too late. Sympathy for the plaintiff was high. The verdict was for the defense.

Sympathy is a natural and powerful emotion. The problem is that when sympathy is overplayed, jurors feel manipulated. When people feel emotionally manipulated, they become angry toward the perceived manipulator.

Let's take a lesson from social media. In the 2014 article, "Experimental Evidence of Massive-Scale Emotional Contagion through Social Networks," researchers Adam Kramer, Jamie Guillory, and Jeffrey Hancock used the social media platform Facebook and its News Feed feature to conduct their study.[12] The Facebook News Feed is a constantly updating list of postings, stories, news links, and photos by the people, groups, and organizations to which a particular Facebook subscriber is connected. In their research, Kramer and his colleagues examined the impact of emotional messages in the News Feed on the behaviors of Facebook subscribers. To conduct their study, they manipulated the emotional messages that appeared on the News Feeds of over 600,000 subscribers and tested whether these messages had an impact on later posting behaviors. The research was conducted by splitting the subscribers into two groups. In one group, positive messages by friends were systematically reduced on the News Feed and in the other, negative messages were reduced. News Feed messages were determined to be positive or negative using a computer software program that sought and identified words deemed positive or negative.

What the researchers found was a significant effect they called, "emotional contagion." In other words, those subscribers who had the positive content of their News Feed reduced posted more negative words themselves and those who had negative content reduced posted more positive words. Interestingly, they also found that people who were exposed to fewer posts that contained any emotion were also less emotionally expressive in their own posts. The results of this research were fascinating and show us how we influence one another's affect, even without face-to-face interaction.

The piece of the research that may be even more fascinating, though, is what happened when the results of the study were released. People. Were. Outraged.

The controversy over this study first involved the issue of informed consent, which the authors addressed in their study by stating that the testing "was consistent with Facebook's Data Use Policy, to which all users agree prior to creating an account on Facebook, constituting informed consent for this research."

---

12. Adam D. Kramer, Jamie E. Guillory, & Jeffery T. Hancock, *Experimental Evidence of Massive-Scale Emotional Contagion through Social Network*, 111 PROCEEDINGS OF THE NATIONAL ACADEMY OF SCIENCES 8788 (2014).

The use of this policy as informed consent has drawn the attention of both the media and the government. The ethics of the experiment were called into question, culminating in a formal complaint to the Federal Trade Commission by Virginia senator Mark Warner.

The second controversial issue—and the real source of upset—involved the nature of the experiment and the fact that so many people were having their emotions intentionally manipulated.

Journalist Violet Blue wrote the following about the experiment in her article "Federal Hot Water for Facebook over Emotional Manipulation" on the website zdnet.com:

> In its "emotional contagion experiment" Facebook tampered with the emotional well-being of 689,003 users to see how their emotions could be controlled; Facebook's hypothesis amounted to "let's see if we can plant unhappiness and make it spread."[13]

The behavior of advertisers elicits the same upset about emotional manipulation. The primary controversy over the Facebook study may be seen as akin to what writer Ryan Calo describes as "market manipulation" in advertising. He expresses concern that consumer protections are being eroded because corporations are collecting personal information about consumers through their digital footprint and using psychology and messaging to target specific interests of a person in marketing. Calo asserts that using consumer's personal information to send messages that influence behavior is harmful.

The point is this: whether on social media, in advertising, in marketing, or in jury trials, people don't like to be manipulated. When they realize that someone is trying to manipulate them, they react. Strongly.

Therefore, despite the defense mantra "beware of the crying juror," I have seen jurors in mock trials weep at the case story and then become strong advocates for the defense. I have also seen jurors express strong anger when they feel that they have been emotionally manipulated as a tactic to get money.

Unfortunately for defendants, little can be done to mitigate the real sympathy people will feel for a permanent injury or the loss of a loved one, a job, or business opportunity. The best way to deal with sympathy is to accept and join in it. However, the defense can remind jurors that the plaintiff's burden is not only to prove how horrible the injuries were, but to first provide the proof that will allow those jurors to look at the defendant and say: "You caused this loss. It is on your head." After all, sympathy can play both ways.

---

13. Violet Blue, *Federal Hot Water for Facebook Over Emotional Manipulation Experiment,* http://www.zdnet.com/federal-hot-water-for-facebook-over-emotional-manipulation-experiment-7000031513 (last visited Jan. 26, 2016).

The power of sympathy in a case is typically in the hands of the plaintiff, and it is a dangerous power to control. There is a balance between presenting the full story of the plaintiff's injuries and turning jurors off by playing too strongly on emotion.

It is more powerful to pepper the liability witnesses' testimony with damage information so jurors make a real connection between what happened and who is to blame.

It is more powerful to pepper the liability witnesses' testimony with damage information so jurors make a real connection between what happened and who is to blame. Sympathy can be a great asset to a plaintiff's case, but if it becomes the focus, the juror may perceive it as a smoke screen for weak liability evidence and thus damage your case.

Questions to Ask Yourself

- Does my case have a strong element of sympathy?
- What impact will that sympathy have on the case?
- Am I overplaying sympathy? Is the other side?
- (*for plaintiff*) Am I coming close to crossing the line of presenting sympathy to such an extent that jurors may feel manipulated?
- (*for plaintiff*) Am I using sympathy to make up for a weak liability story?

1.9 Distinguish the Law from Jurors' Sense of Justice

During a presentation I made about jury selection at a national seminar for public defenders, one of the attendees said she believed jurors didn't understand what "beyond a reasonable doubt" means. She held this belief because she couldn't understand why jurors send her clients to jail after hours of deliberating. If they have to deliberate that long, then they must have doubt. Right?

This public defender's comment caused me to consider how I have seen the burden of proof and its associated law managed by jurors when making verdict decisions.

So why does this defender lose her cases after people spend time deliberating? I think it is unlikely that the culprit was a lack of understanding the specific burden of proof instruction. It's possible, but unlikely. Instead, it is more likely that jurors without a reasonable doubt have to spend time convincing other jurors of their perspective, or the jurors may simply have been conscientious in going through the evidence before sending a person to jail.

But there may be another reason as well.

While in these trials the evidence proved that the defendants did indeed perpetrate the "crime," many were acquitted because the jurors felt that the laws were unfair. This wasn't a case of jurors not understanding. It was one of them understanding all too well.

In his 2004 article, "In Defense of Jury Nullification Litigation," Paul Butler describes the origin of the jury nullification phenomenon, in which jurors will consciously render a verdict contrary to legal standards because they disagree with the law. He describes criminal trials in the 1800s when citizens were arrested and tried for helping to free slaves. While in these trials the evidence proved that the defendants did indeed perpetrate the "crime," many were acquitted because the jurors felt that the laws were unfair. This wasn't a case of jurors not understanding. It was one of them understanding all too well.[14]

I see the same issue in civil trials.

While presenting at another seminar on the psychology of jurors with civil trial litigators and judges, I provided some of my own research findings to the crowd. Over the years, I have asked thousands of jurors to answer this question:

> *In a trial, is it most important that the jury makes a decision that*
>
> *a) follows the rules set by the judge?*
>
> *b) the jury believes is fair?*

---

14. Paul Butler, *In Defense of Jury Nullification*, 3 Litigation 46 (2004).

While most of the lawyers on the panel were not surprised, some of the judges were dismayed to see that 61 percent of the sample I had collected indicated it is more important for the jury to make a decision it believes is fair than it is for the jury to follow the rules. That sounds like jury nullification to me.

A senior judge on the panel raised his hand and asked me a very legitimate question. "Well," he said, "are they in conflict?" I pondered the question for a moment and responded, "That depends on who is making that decision."

It is a simple fact that there are some jurors who simply do not trust authority systems and therefore will not be compelled by what someone in an official-looking robe tells them is right or wrong. In fact, for some, that robe may lead to more distrust. Overall, these jurors' life experiences and sense of justice will take precedent over any complex law or rule.

I routinely see jurors interpret the law in a way that supports their idea of "fair," going about the process backwards. Fair dictates their interpretation of the law. The law doesn't guide their interpretation of fair.

There are also times when jurors simply aren't properly educated on the law. They aren't provided clear connections between the technical legal language on the verdict form and how their decisions sound in their own vernacular. Without a deeper understanding of what it all means, the jurors can simply misinterpret the law rather than necessarily disagree with it.

As a result, I routinely see jurors interpret the law in a way that supports their idea of "fair," going about the process backwards. Fair dictates their interpretation of the law. The law doesn't guide their interpretation of fair.

This happened on a case I was working on in which healthcare providers were being sued for failing to diagnose an infection. The day after her visit to the emergency room, the plaintiff went into septic shock. She lived, but lost all four of her limbs at the elbows and knees—*all four.*

During an agonizing weeks-long trial, the jurors learned the symptoms the plaintiff presented to the defendants, the test results, and the advice from the specialists who were consulted. Based on interviews we conducted with the jurors after the trial, we learned that the jurors understood that while the infection was, in fact, missed, it was reasonably missed because of its unusual presentation. The jurors understood that the doctors went through a rigorous and thorough process, made a reasonable conclusion, and had a reasonable follow-up plan in place. So, the jurors decided, there was no medical negligence.

Did I mention that the plaintiff lost all four limbs?

Through those interviews, we also learned a few other things. First, there was one juror who flat out admitted he decided that the plaintiff should collect damages as soon as he saw her in the courthouse and before jury selection began. Of course, despite repeated questions designed to elicit such a sentiment, this juror hid his bias from counsel and the court during the voir dire process. He simply could not let someone with that level of injury leave her trial without money. He was going to make sure she got something.

For other jurors, we learned about the struggle they went through in their deliberations. They were faced with a conundrum: how could they make sure the plaintiff gets money for her unthinkable outcome from a missed diagnosis without punishing medical providers who weren't medically negligent? They found a way to satisfy their conflict through the verdict form.

On the verdict form, there was a way that the plaintiff could recover damages other than through negligence. That is, if the jurors found that the medical providers failed to provide adequate informed consent, they could determine that was a cause of her outcome and award damages even without medical negligence. So the jurors decided that they could find the defendants not negligent, but then find that they had failed to provide informed consent. The jurors had rationalized their finding that the medical providers failed to inform the plaintiff about treatment options for infection, even though the providers determined she didn't have one. In their minds, they interpreted the legal principle to suit their concept of justice.

With that, the jurors were able to award a verdict worthy of newspaper headlines without finding the defendants negligent.

Of course, understanding how to properly educate the jurors on legal principles and how they connect to the verdict form questions is critical. This is a delicate dance of both staying within the courtroom rules regarding the extent to which you may address the law and avoiding inundating the jurors with overly complex concepts. The point is to make the connections simple.

Regardless, we cannot dismiss the reality that sometimes jurors see the law and fairness to be in conflict and will therefore ignore the law completely. A case I worked on in Detroit comes to mind. In this case, an EMT molested a minor in the back of an ambulance. The EMT was in jail, and the minor, through her family, was suing the ambulance company for failing to prevent the incident. The only *legal* issue was whether the driver of the ambulance acted reasonably based on what he could perceive from the driver's seat. The defense wanted to understand how jurors would deal with this law, given the story.

In our focus group, we learned that the jurors understood the legal principle and did not see that the driver did anything wrong. In fact, they felt sympathy for the position he was put in. It didn't matter. They weren't buying the argument that the ambulance company was faultless. The company hired a child molester. It didn't matter what the law said. It didn't matter that the perpetrator had neither a history of such behavior nor a criminal record. That company hired him. It put him in a position to be alone with the minor, and he had sexual contact with a minor. End of story. The case could not be settled, and the team was forced to go to trial. Unfortunately, for the defense, the real jury felt the same way.

So let's get back to our public defender. Maybe, just maybe, she is losing cases because her jurors are focused on their concept of "justice" for their community. Maybe, just maybe, even if they had a doubt that the accused committed the crime at issue, if they see having this person out of the community serves the greater good, that, to them, is more important than following the judge's instructions.

Justice, after all, is in the eye of the juror.

Questions to Ask Yourself

- What are the legal principles that jurors need to understand in my case?

- Am I addressing the legal principles and how they connect to the verdict form in way the jurors understand?

- Where may jurors see a "justice" in this case?

- Where may jurors sense of justice conflict with the legal principles?

- How is the way I tell my case story addressing the jurors' sense of justice?

1.10 Consider that Common Sense Isn't Always Common

I hear it in real trials. I hear it in mock trials. Almost every single one. What is *it*? It is the following statement: "Ladies and Gentlemen, you just have to use your common sense to find [*insert what we want the jurors to find here*]."

F. L. van Holthoorn and David Olson (1987) defined common sense as the "knowledge, judgment, and taste which is more or less universal and which is held more or less without reflection or argument."[15] So when you talk about common sense, you are talking about what you believe to be apparent and presupposed by all human beings. As a result, you communicate implications to a person when you tell them that something is "common sense." It provides the message that said belief should be known to them, intuitively. But what message do you send when it isn't?

The fact of the matter is that common sense isn't always so "common," and what you may consider common sense may not relate to the sensibilities of a particular juror.

The words you use and the insinuations you project through those words can have a profound impact on the way jurors view you and your case. Be careful about making assumptions about what someone else would or should consider obvious.

While this can be true in any kind of case, I particularly find it in complex cases in which the issues make it difficult for jurors to make any sense of the case, let alone a "common" kind. I remember, in particular, some very complex contract litigation that was chock full of accounting principles and financial complexities. In mock trial deliberations, knee-deep in the information, jurors laughingly referred to a comment made by one of the attorneys. That attorney told the jurors they would only need to apply their common sense to the facts of the case and the answers to the verdict form would be clear. After one juror referenced that comment, the rest joined in on the laughter. While the sense of the evidence may have been common to the attorney, it certainly wasn't to the jurors.

The words you use and the insinuations you project through those words can have a profound impact on the way jurors view you and your case. Be careful about making assumptions about what someone else would or should consider obvious.

The danger is this: if you are telling a juror to use his common sense to agree with you, and he sees the story differently, you not only have someone who may not see things as you do, but you also have someone you have just alienated. The end result

---

15. Frits L. van Holthoon & David R. Olson, *Common Sense: The Foundations for Social Science* (1987).

is that you may have created a stronger adversary than otherwise. You have insulted his common sense because he disagrees with your position.

It all makes common sense, doesn't it?

Questions to Ask Yourself

- Am I asking jurors to use their common sense in my case presentation?

- To what extent am I alienating people who may not see common sense as I do?

- Is my "common sense" argument universal and compelling enough to take the risk of alienating someone?

1.11 Use Disturbing Evidence Only When Necessary

The Kermit Gosnell abortion trial made national news with the tagline "House of Horrors." Gosnell was convicted of the murder of three infants who were born alive during abortion procedures he conducted at his Philadelphia clinic. The news tagline was fitting, considering the graphic photographs and testimony that the jurors had to endure, describing babies born alive only to later be killed by Gosnell and other members of his staff.

Reporters contacted me to comment on the trial and the sense that after days upon days of seeing and hearing about horrible things, the jurors seemed not to visibly react as strongly to the gruesome evidence as they did when the trial first began. One reporter wanted to know whether that meant the jurors weren't being impacted by the evidence anymore and whether the graphic nature of the testimony was, in fact, beginning to backfire on the prosecution. My answer: "The evidence is likely still quite impactful, but it very well may become impactful in a way it was not intended to be."

Because many of the cases I work on involve personal injuries, I have been exposed to some pretty awful accidents with unimaginable injuries. The photographic evidence in these cases can be extremely difficult to view, particularly when the accidents involve children.

There are few universal truths in trials, but this is one of them: most jurors don't want to be forced to look at horrible photos of real injuries. At all. This should be the foundational assumption when you are making decisions of what to show and what not to show. Therefore, it is critical to stop and consider what the jurors really need to see and how much of it they need to see.

Graphic evidence certainly affects jury decisions, as proven empirically by researchers Douglas, Lyon, and Ogloff in a 1997 study on mock jurors in a murder trial. One group of juror participants, used as a control group, was not shown a picture of the murder victim at all. The two experimental groups were shown either a black-and-white or color photo of the victim after the crime. The results were that the experimental groups shown the photographs were twice as likely to render a guilty verdict. All of the juror participants who were shown the photographs also reported emotional distress after seeing the images.

There are few universal truths in trials, but this is one of them: most jurors don't want to be forced to look at horrible photos of real injuries. At all.

Considering the disparate decisions resulting from the same fact pattern and the emotional impact the images had on the jurors, the researchers discussed concern about whether the photographs were probative or prejudicial.[16]

---

16. K. S. Douglas, D. R. Lyon & J. R. P. Ogloff, *The Impact of Graphic Photographic Evidence on Mock Jurors' Decisions in a Murder Trial: Probative or Prejudicial?*, 21 LAW AND HUMAN BEHAVIOR 485 (1997).

National Institute for Trial Advocacy

This question was likely an issue for the Gosnell trial as well. For Gosnell, though, the photographs of the injuries were important physical evidence of how the infants died. Did the photographs cause distress? Of course they did. But they had an evidentiary purpose that the jurors could understand.

The results of the research by Douglas and his colleagues are not surprising. The finding that disturbing images impact juror emotion and decisions is intuitive. As a result, plaintiffs in jury trials feel the urge to show the jurors the gruesome aftermath of an accident to bring into the courtroom the true horror of what happened. Emotionally distressed jurors may be more likely to award higher damages, after all. Bright and Goodman (2006) studied the impact of gruesome evidence on jury decision-making and found, similarly to the 1997 study, that showing graphic photographs does increase the conviction rate in murder trials and also measurably increases juror anger, not just distress.[17]

So in a civil trial, when the jurors decide that the defendant is at fault, these images can increase their anger and, in turn, increase damages. But what happens in civil cases when the jurors decide that the defendant is not to blame? Where does the anger go?

This issue touches on two decision points for litigators in any case involving a physical injury that is unpleasant to see, whether criminal or civil.

In a civil trial, when the jurors decide that the defendant is at fault, these images can increase their anger and, in turn, increase damages. But what happens in civil cases when the jurors decide that the defendant is not to blame? Where does the anger go?

The first decision is whether to show the graphic evidence at all. There are times when presenting such evidence is ill advised. When such upsetting images don't help a jury make their decision, jurors can actually direct their anger toward whoever is forcing them to look at the images. I have heard jurors complain that pictures and disturbing testimony was simply purposed to manipulate their emotions so the plaintiffs could get what they wanted. In those instances, the jurors did get upset, but not in the way plaintiffs intended.

This is an important consideration where graphic evidence neither tells the story of liability nor explains a plaintiff's ordeal in a relevant manner. I remember a case in Oklahoma in which there was a carbon monoxide leak into an apartment building, killing the inhabitants of some of the apartments. The bodies were found several weeks later in a scene akin to a horror movie. Did the jurors need to see those bodies in varying states of decomposition to determine who was at fault for a leak in the

---

17. David A. Bright & Jane Goodman-Delahuty, *Gruesome Evidence and Emotion: Anger, Blame and Jury Decision-Making*, 30 LAW AND HUMAN BEHAVIOR 183 (2006).

boiler? No, they didn't. Did the images provide any kind of story about pain and suffering that the victims went through? No, they didn't. The horror piece of the horror scene happened after the victims died—it was the natural process of what happens to a body post-mortem.

If you determine that graphic images are indeed relevant and important to provide, you have a second decision to make. How much to show? It is often unwise to show upsetting images repeatedly. This was likely the issue those reporters were concerned about in the Gosnell trial. The pictures were relevant for decision-making, but may have gotten to the point of being overused.

When you overuse any dramatic evidence, you run a risk. First, jurors will become desensitized to it. While the images will continue to be disturbing, the shock value will abate. Second, showing these kinds of images repeatedly may begin to cross that line in jurors' minds from important evidence to emotional manipulation. This is a critical line. Be aware of it.

If you are going to show photos of a terrible injury, first give jurors a warning. Tell them that you are about to show an upsetting image and more importantly, tell them *why* it is so important to your case for you to cause them the distress it will produce. Show the evidence only as many times as absolutely needed. Just once often suffices. If you need to refer to it again, do so orally. If the image was truly that disturbing, the jurors won't have forgotten about it. To the contrary, it likely will be seared in their brains.

I also advise that if graphic and disturbing images are not absolutely critical to your case, do not show them at trial. In fact, on more than one occasion (including that carbon monoxide case in Oklahoma), I have advised attorneys to put the images in an envelope and tell the jurors that the pictures are available, but give the jurors the choice of whether to look for themselves. In truth, the jurors usually can't help themselves. Curiosity abounds. Someone looks. And when that happens, they are unlikely to hold their own decision to look against you. After all, you warned them.

Questions to Ask Yourself

- How upsetting is the graphic evidence in my case?
- Is that evidence directly relevant to the verdict questions?
- Do I need to show the evidence more than once?
- Do I risk desensitizing the jury to my key evidence by showing it multiple times?
- Am I better served by giving the evidence to the jurors to look at if they choose instead of presenting it in the courtroom?

1.12 Turn Your Perspective Outside In

A highlight of my career as a jury consultant occurred during a seminar I was presenting with one of my clients, a senior litigator of a national law firm. He said to the crowd: "Jury consultants like Melissa can give us a different perspective on the case. She essentially lets us know if we have a good case or if we are just absorbed in our own B.S." Regardless of the fact that I had to chuckle at this description of my job, this client made a good and important point that all attorneys should consider when preparing their cases.

It is extremely difficult to step back and understand what someone outside the team may perceive when viewing the case for the first time and from a ten-thousand-foot view. Regardless of its difficulty, that step back is critical when presenting a case to a jury.

The fact of the matter is that after years of being involved in a case, a trial team no longer has an outside perspective. Instead, by the time a case makes it to trial, the team has typically been so involved in the nuts and bolts and minute details of the legal and factual issues it gets stuck inside its own perspective. It is extremely difficult to step back and understand what someone outside the team may perceive when viewing the case for the first time and from a ten-thousand-foot view. Regardless of its difficulty, that step back is critical when presenting a case to a jury.

We can take some lessons from the field of marketing in this regard. In their book, *Strategy from Outside In, Profiting from Customer Value,* George Day and Christine Moorman discuss how successful companies start with an external market orientation and focus on trends and desires of customers as the starting point of designing their market strategy.[18] They call it "outside-in" thinking. This is in contrast to an "inside-out" strategy, which looks at the company's existing resources and ways to streamline operations to create business successes. Day and Moorman posit that while an inside-out approach can create short-term gains, the internal focus limits a company's ability to notice and adapt to market changes. They cite the example of the automobile manufacturer Toyota, which shifted its focus away from meeting customer needs toward the internal goal of beating a competitor, General Motors. As a result of its focus on the wrong goal, quality suffered and sales dropped. Toyota lost customers.

Best Buy, on the other hand, was cited as a good example of outside-in thinking. During a time when personal computer manufacturers were driving down costs and cutting back services, Best Buy saw an increased demand for home and business support. It saw the growth of social media and decided to act on what the public

---

18. George S. Day & Christine Moorman, *Strategy from the Outside In: Profiting from Customer Value* (2010).

was telling it. Best Buy created the Geek Squad, a traveling information technology support service, and Twelpforce, a customer service platform leveraging the social media networking site Twitter. It worked.

The same concept of applying an outside-in strategy at the onset is critical for a successful trial. It becomes more and more difficult to retroactively apply a new strategy the longer you have been entrenched in the strategy with which you began—even if that strategy isn't working. It is especially true if the strategy is focused solely on legal principles and not the perspective of ordinary citizens.

The best outside perspective is from potential jurors themselves. To get this viewpoint, mock trials or focus groups allow you to present the case to a representative sample of eligible jurors. In the right case, when there is a lot at stake, getting the perspective of members of your venue's community can be eye-opening—and well worth any additional costs it might entail. There is no better way to take a step outside of your own perspective than to hear a group of ordinary citizens discussing their opinions of your case and your arguments.

In fact, I am seeing a trend with litigators conducting these kinds of exercises earlier in litigation so that juror perspectives lead the development of trial strategy, taking those perspectives into account as the case moves through the discovery process. In other words, like Best Buy successfully did, these litigators are shaping the litigation process using an outside-in strategy.

Does this mean you need a jury consultant or a mock trial for every case you have going to trial? No. What it means is that you should get some sort of outside perspective—whatever form that may take. Do I recommend using a jury consultant? When you can. Jury consultants are trained to provide an unbiased perspective (unlike your mother or husband who want to encourage you . . . usually). The attention of a good jury consultant is focused on those people who do not know the law and who you, as a lawyer, may not encounter in your daily life. Yet these are the folks who make decisions about your case.

In essence, finding a way to turn your view of your case from inside out to outside in could very well be the difference between making a winning argument and making an argument that is, in the eloquent words of my client, "absorbed in [your] own B.S."

Questions to Ask Yourself

- At what point in the litigation process did I start considering my jurors?

- Have I become too involved in the case or too wedded to my own perception of it?

- Considering the size and nature of the case, what is my best way of getting a reliable outside perspective?

- Does this case warrant a jury consultant or a jury research exercise?

PART TWO

CHOOSING TRIAL STRATEGIES

2.1   Use Opposing Counsel's Momentum to Your Advantage

The art of Sumo wrestling employs a technique called *yobi modoshi*, a move in which a wrestler uses his charging opponent's momentum to propel his opponent down. The same conceptual tactic is a useful tool, when used wisely, when dealing with damaging evidence or powerful case themes against your own clients at trial.

The concept of stealing thunder is one familiar to litigators. The manner in which most of us consider stealing thunder is by presenting damaging evidence first, or head-on, to mitigate the power it provides the adversary. In the right circumstances, you may also deflate the persuasive punch of an adversary's effective argument or case theme simply by embracing the momentum of that theme and turning it to your advantage. In this case, though, it isn't about minimizing its power. It is about changing the direction of that power.

If it is working for them, make it work for you.

In the right circumstances, you may also deflate the persuasive punch of an adversary's effective argument or case theme simply by embracing the momentum of that theme and turning it to your advantage.

I remember a medical malpractice trial in a small town in Iowa, the plaintiff, a forty-something All-American athlete father sued his oncologist for failing to accurately diagnose his rare form of cancer. At trial, the plaintiff was clearly in the end stages of his disease. He appeared in the courtroom frail, emaciated, and with a large visible scar across the top of his head from a recent brain surgery. I was working with the defense.

Plaintiff's counsel started trial in full force, weaving his theme of the defendant doctor as the "captain of the ship" into his interaction with the jurors as early as voir dire. Plaintiff's counsel argued that as the "captain of the ship," the defendant was responsible for correctly diagnosing the disease and directing the course of treatment by all other providers. If the "captain" did not find the accurate diagnosis, he could not direct the crew to the treatment that would have saved the plaintiff's life.

According to a shadow jury we employed to watch the proceedings each day and provide feedback on trial events, the theme was effective. Jurors evaluated the defendant's actions through the "captain of the ship" analogy. The theme became a mantra for the case, and it was dangerous to the defense for such a resonating theme to be associated only with the plaintiff's case.

The plaintiff was gaining ground, and we had to do something fast. I told counsel that fighting against the momentum the "captain" theme had gained would be fruitless and counterproductive. It had gained too much power. The team agreed. Therefore, we developed a strategy congruent with *yobi modoshi*. We got on the "captain of the ship" bandwagon.

The defense also wove the "captain of the ship" analogy into its questioning of the remaining witnesses, as well as into closing statements. The defense argued that in a situation in which a life is at stake, the "captain" does not sit around and wait. He makes decisions. He acts. With only one course of treatment available, no matter what kind of cancer the plaintiff had, this "captain" decided to fight the disease instead of continuing with diagnostic testing. The defense declared, "Yes, the defendant was the 'captain of the ship,' and, as the 'captain,' he made the tough decisions—the right decisions." The jury returned a verdict in favor of the defense.

What makes stealing thunder with damaging evidence so effective is that it changes the context in which the jurors learn about and perceive the evidence. Stealing the thunder of case themes is also very effective if you use it cautiously and strategically. If there is a powerful force in the courtroom, finding a way to use its momentum in your own case is one of the most powerful strategies you can employ.

In essence, even in the battle of the courtroom, sometimes it is not best to fight against effective mantras. Sometimes it is more effective to simply go with (or better yet, redirect) the flow.

Questions to Ask Yourself

- What themes are opposing counsel employing?

- How effective is that theme for opposing counsel?

- Can I adopt and reframe that theme in a way that works for my case?

- How can adopting opposing counsel's theme backfire on me?

2.2   Validate the Jury's Visceral Response

I was working with the plaintiff on a motorcycle accident death case in New Jersey. While the defendant's liability was pretty clear, the plaintiff had a problem. The decedent's post-mortem blood alcohol level measured beyond the legal limit. My client, needless to say, was concerned. How could he get jurors to disregard the blood alcohol reading when telling the story of what happened? My answer: "You can't."

In *Gut Reactions: A Perceptual Theory of Emotion*, Jesse Prinz describes the embodied appraisal theory. This theory espouses that strong visceral reactions include responses from both the mind *and* the body. He explains:

> First of all, they [gut reactions] are perceptions of changes in the body, but, through the body, they also allow us to literally perceive danger, loss, and other matters of concern.[1]

Prinz's explanation of the essence of visceral or "gut" reactions helps us understand why such responses are so difficult to overcome. People feel these reactions physically and interpret them cognitively. It is extremely difficult, if not near impossible, to overcome a response that is both physical and cognitive with tactics that are solely cognitive.

It is more effective to join jurors in the natural reaction. Go where the jurors are, then help them see a different perspective from their vantage point.

Therefore, in trials that involve strong visceral response, like the motorcycle accident case, trying to avoid or ignore jurors' visceral reaction is unwise. In fact, if you tell jurors that something they find critical is not important or you otherwise fail to account for how they naturally feel, you will cause jurors to close themselves off to anything else you have to say. You become a challenge to their natural instincts instead of the voice of truth or reason.

Instead, it is more effective to join jurors in the natural reaction. Go where the jurors are, then help them see a different perspective from *their* vantage point.

In the motorcycle accident case, without getting into too many gruesome details, the blood sample had to be taken from a body that was in several pieces, as unfortunately sometimes happens with motorcycle accidents. According to our expert, for the alcohol level to have read as high as it did, the decedent, who had been on the road for about two hours, would have had to have consumed so much alcohol before he got on his bike that there was absolutely no way he would have

---

1. Jesse J. Prinz, *Gut Reactions: A Perceptual Theory of Emotion* (2004).

been able to stand, let alone ride a motorcycle without incident for two hours on a busy highway. The test results, while powerful for the defense, didn't match up to the story.

I advised counsel to say something like this:

> When I first heard about the case and learned about Mr. X's blood alcohol reading, I thought to myself: "An elevated blood alcohol level? Drunk driver! Case closed!"

At trial, this joined with the jurors' visceral reactions and got them nodding. Then, counsel continued:

> But, ladies and gentlemen, we are here in court for a reason. That reason is because, as I looked more closely at the case, I saw the evidence that you will see and you will hear, and something didn't seem quite right. When I looked more closely, I realized that science is only exact when it is performed exactly right . . . .

By joining the jurors' natural reactions instead of coming out of the gate saying the incongruent evidence "doesn't matter" or "is wrong," this lawyer got jurors to listen to, instead of ignore, his messages. While the case did settle before the end of trial, interviews with the jurors revealed that the approach had worked. Jurors agreed that despite their initial reaction to the blood alcohol results, they felt they could not rely on them and were leaning favorably toward the plaintiff's side of the case.

Questions to Ask Yourself

- What are the issues in my case that are likely to produce a strong visceral response?

- Will that visceral response be helpful to me, or do I have to overcome it?

- How do I acknowledge the jurors' visceral responses instead of dismissing them?

2.3   Calculate the Impact of Omissions on Trust

I had the pleasure of performing some pro bono work for the defense in a criminal trial in Philadelphia with high media exposure. The case involved the shooting of a police officer on November 27, 1966. On that day in 1966, the defendant perpetrator was in the process of breaking into a beauty supply store with the intent to rob it. He was approached by a twenty-three-year-old rookie cop. The defendant shot the young officer twice, rendering him paraplegic.

Fast-forward forty years to 2007. The officer, in his sixties, died of sepsis caused by a urinary tract infection, a known complication of paralysis. The defendant had been arrested, tried, and convicted of *attempted* murder when the shooting occurred. He served his sentence and was released. In 2007, after the officer died, he was arrested again in relation to the same shooting. This time, the charge was murder.

What the jurors had to decide was whether the shots fired in 1966 were the cause of the officer's death over forty years later. The prosecution had to show an unbroken causal chain of events from the shooting to the death. The jurors were not told that the defendant had already served a jail sentence for the original shooting. The judge ruled that this was irrelevant to the question of cause. Cause was cause.

A plethora of lessons came out of this fascinating trial, but one stood out above the rest. It came from the prosecutor's opening. At the beginning of the trial, the prosecutor started with the story of the shooting that happened on November 27. She said, "On November 27, (the defendant) shot (the young police officer)." She repeated the date, just as written, several times. Notice anything missing? In the entire opening, not once did she mention the year. Not once.

I am quite sure that her intended message was that the year did not matter. Whether the death happened a minute later, a week later, a year later, or forty years later, if the shooting caused the death, it was murder. But she didn't say that. She just left out the year. Instead of the intended message, the message that came across was that the prosecution was willing to withhold important parts of the story to make its case. Regardless of whether the prosecution thought the year was an important enough part of the case to mention, the jurors certainly did.

Watching the prosecutor's opening in this criminal case reinforced some key strategic principles that apply to the civil arena. Specifically, it is typically inadvisable to withhold key pieces of information that the other side will bring out. It unfailingly rubs jurors the wrong way and leads them to lose trust in you as a speaker. Especially when the other side reveals what you omitted.

Sometimes we need to take strategic risks. In doing so, we have to be sure they are going to work and that they are not going to damage our position.

The concept of audience trust in a speaker was studied by Louis Guenin, who presented his findings in the article, "Intellectual Honesty."[2] Much akin to what I observed in that Philadelphia courtroom, Guenin states that to engage trust, a speaker must be perceived as both telling the truth and telling it completely. The audience may perceive withholding important information with the same kind of skepticism as providing outright false information.

Sometimes we need to take strategic risks. In doing so, we have to be sure they are going to work and that they are not going to damage our position. In this case, the prosecutor's omission in the opening set a tone that the prosecution could not overcome. The prosecution rested. The defense presented no witnesses. The verdict: not guilty.

Questions to Ask Yourself

- What information am I choosing not to tell the jurors?
- Will the information I omit be brought up by the other side?
- Do I run the risk of losing the trust of my jurors by leaving key information out?
- How can I address my bad fact effectively instead?

---

2. Louis M. Guenin, *Intellectual Honesty*, 145 SYNTHESE 177 (2005).

2.4   Keep Key Points from Getting Lost in the Middle

I have seen it more times than I can count. Well-intentioned and well-organized trial attorneys present their openings, closings, witnesses, and witness examinations in a clear, logical order. They make the introductions first; provide background and context; make the key points; and then tie it together. It makes perfect sense. It is well organized. It has a nice flow . . . and too often the key points lose their punch by getting lost in the middle.

In the psychology of learning, there are two concepts that every trial attorney should know well and integrate into every aspect of trial: primacy and recency. These concepts mean that people remember most what they hear first and what they hear last. For example, if you heard ten words and were asked to recite them aloud, you would probably have an easy time stating the first few and the last few, but you would probably have the most difficulty in recalling the words in the middle.

In the psychology of learning, there are two concepts that every trial attorney should know well and integrate into every aspect of trial: primacy and recency. These concepts mean that people remember most what they hear first and what they hear last.

A potential explanation for the primacy and recency effects was studied by Rundus and Atkinson (1970), who, after studying the recall of a rehearsed list of items, found that items provided first were rehearsed most repeatedly and those provided last had the benefit of closeness in time to the recall.[3] Research on this subject has shown the influence of primacy and recency in academics, memory of musical composition, politics, and just about every other subject area that involves human learning. The concepts are universal and pervasive and should not be overlooked in litigation.

In the practical world, primacy and recency have been used in political campaigns, as studied by Costas Panagopoulos and reported in his 2011 article in *Political Behavior*.[4] Panagopoulos found in a randomized field experiment in Rochester, New York, that the key political message delivered both at the very beginning and very end of a campaign had significant effect on voter decisions. The same idea applies to jurors at a trial.

What I have seen in my practice is that primacy and recency not only affect the retention, but also the impact of an argument. Specifically, if you present a message out of the natural order of how a story is typically told, it will grab attention. The audience is not expecting it.

---

3. R. C. Atkinson, *Rehearsal Processes in Free Recall: A Procedure for Direct Observation*, 9 JOURNAL OF VERBAL LEARNING AND VERBAL BEHAVIOR 99 (1970).
4. Costas Panagopoulos, *Timing Is Everything? Primacy and Recency Effects in Voter Mobilization Campaigns*, 33 POLITICAL BEHAVIOR 79 (2011).

What I have seen in my practice is that primacy and recency not only affect the retention, but also the impact of an argument.

Primacy and recency can have a substantial impact on the effectiveness of an opening, a witness examination, a closing, a case. I have seen great trial attorneys make meaningful and impactful statements in openings before introducing themselves. It makes sense to me. Why waste those first precious moments, when juror attention is the greatest, on telling your name instead of your point? You can get to the name later.

The idea is also relevant when presenting a witness at trial: most often, you spend the first critical moments introducing the witness, describing her job and educational background, etc. By the time you get to the meat of her testimony, it is ten, twenty, thirty, or more minutes into the questioning. At this point, you have lost both the jurors' undivided attention and the benefits of the primacy effect. The important points lose the impact they would have had if they were revealed coming out of the gate.

Of course, in some instances, you must provide that background information first to qualify the witness as an expert or set a foundation for key testimony before the panel. The rules are the rules. In these instances, when you can't have the expert give the conclusion first, take advantage of breaks to provide the key punches in a newly refreshed setting, where you have reestablished primacy.

During a CLE panel with experienced trial attorneys, a fellow panelist and trial attorney demonstrated the concept of primacy perfectly. He presented the following testimony taken from the transcript of a murder trial in which a man was on trial for hiring someone to kill his wife. The alleged hit man was on the stand. These were the first two questions from the prosecuting attorney:

Q: Were you hired to kill Mrs. X?

A: Yes.

Q: Who hired you?

A: (*pointing at the defendant*) Mr. X.

The prosecutor provided the background information and context after the punch, but the jurors didn't need to hear much more after that.

Points made last also have a resounding effect. I was a member of the defense team in a product liability trial, and in the middle of the cross-examination of the plaintiff's key expert on product defect, I had noticed that for the expert's ideas to apply, some critical assumptions had to be made about the product user's behavior that were not realistic. After a brief caucus with the lead attorney, we developed a plan to grab the jurors' attention. Examination resumed and, per our plan, just when it seemed as though he was about to finish his questioning of the expert, the attorney paused, then asked two more questions:

Q: For any of your opinions to be true, we have to assume *X*, right?

A: Yes.

Q: There is no evidence of *X* in this case, is there?

A: No.

That final point hung heavily in the air, drawing attention to the fact that assumption *X*, in fact, did not happen and, therefore, the expert's points were moot.

Questions to Ask Yourself

- What are the key, overarching messages I want the jurors to understand and remember?

- Where am I putting those key messages in my case presentations?

- Am I putting the most important and compelling messages first and last to maximize their impact?

2.5 Defendants: Fight Liability

In a Texas trucking accident case, there was no question about who caused the collision. A truck changed lanes, and the driver didn't see a passenger car in his blind spot. He hit the back corner of the car and sent it spinning into a guardrail. What caused the accident wasn't an issue in this case. But the damages certainly were.

After the accident, the plaintiff walked away, refusing medical treatment on the scene. She later claimed that she had sustained a severe head trauma and was rendered almost completely disabled. The defendant trucking company disagreed.

I have found the following to be almost universally true: damage awards are higher in cases where the defense admits liability than they are when the defense does not, even in those cases in which liability is clear.

I have seen several cases in which the cause of an incident seems clear, but what the damages are and, especially, what they are worth, is not. In these cases, I often conduct mock trials with surrogate jurors to see how members of the community perceive liability and value the case. In these exercises, I have found the following to be almost universally true: damage awards are higher in cases where the defense admits liability than they are when the defense does not, even in those cases in which liability is clear.

It seems counterintuitive. At least it did to me at first. Wouldn't jurors have more respect for a defendant that owned up to its responsibility, especially if that defendant is a company? Wouldn't a defendant taking proper responsibility for a mistake abate the juror emotion that can serve to increase damages? One would think. But in most cases, it doesn't.

Instead, the opposite holds true—when jurors only deliberate about damages and injuries without needing to consider liability, sympathy runs high and damages skyrocket. When liability is contested, however, jurors are forced to discuss the defendant by addressing the liability evidence. They become more aware of the defendant's perspective and, as a result, feel empathetic toward that defendant, even knowing that the defendant did something wrong. They not only think about what the plaintiff may deserve to receive, but what the defendant deserves to pay given the circumstances from both vantage points.

While the effect of this phenomenon is intensified when the defendant is an individual, it also applies to corporations. After all, the actions of a corporate defendant are the actions of the individuals within it.

Take our trucking accident, for instance. While the defendant was a corporation, the target of the liability discussion was the individual truck driver. In mock trial deliberations, jurors spoke about the driver and whether his behavior was egregious or whether he simply made a mistake that could "happen to you or me."

Notwithstanding the higher expectations they held of professional drivers than of others on the road to avoid accidents, jurors recognized that mistakes happen.

Their discussions allowed them to see the events through the perspective of the driver, and while they held him liable and awarded damages, their empathy with the driver counterbalanced their sympathy for the plaintiff. This counterbalance influenced damage-related discussions. Jurors were willing to consider the defense perspective on damages and the possibility that the plaintiff was overreaching with her claim.

In this case, defense counsel had nothing to gain by denying the manner in which the accident happened, so he didn't. Instead, counsel conceded the facts as they were and simply told the jurors that they had to determine whether what happened rose to the legal definition of negligence. The defense was realistic in its expectations: the jurors would find liability. But giving the jurors the opportunity to discuss the driver's perspective could only benefit the defendants when the jurors valued the case. As predicted, the jurors found the defendant liable, but awarded a fraction of the damages requested by plaintiff.

Therefore, when it comes to matters where you face a question of whether to admit liability, the rule of thumb for defendants is to avoid doing so. In the absence of facts, jurors will create the liability story for themselves, so you need to consider whether what they could imagine is truly less damaging than what actually happened. If it is, it is best that you find a way to resolve the case before it gets into a jury's hands.

If the liability facts really are so damaging, you are likely facing a punitive damages claim anyway—so the worst of the story will inevitably get out regardless of what you have conceded.

Questions to Ask Yourself (as Defense Counsel)

- Am I likely to lose on liability?

- Will jurors empathize with my defendant, even if I am likely to lose on liability?

- How can I tell my story in a way that walks the line between maximizing empathy toward my defendant and overreaching on a liability defense?

- Is my liability evidence so damaging that I am better off leaving the liability story to jurors' imaginations?

2.6 Plaintiffs: Look Critically at Consortium Claims

A few years back, I was working for the plaintiff on a case in which a woman had severe leg injuries after being run over by a bus in Atlantic City. Her leg sustained terrible damage from being trapped under the weight of the bus's front tire. She had recovered, albeit with a loss of a good deal of the independence and athleticism she once enjoyed. She was a very likable person and a good witness.

Part of the case was her husband's claim for loss of consortium. So when interviewing the couple about the case, I wanted to take a pulse on that claim. I asked the husband what has changed for him since his wife's accident. "Well," he said, "she used to be very active and out and about. Now she is here all the time. I don't get my alone time as much." My first order of business after that meeting: make sure the loss of consortium claim was out of the case before he was deposed.

A claim of a spouse after a severe injury to his or her counterpart can be very powerful in a trial . . . but not *every trial*. There are times when jurors raise an eyebrow at a spouse who asks to be awarded money over someone else's injury. I have heard many a juror in mock trial deliberations exclaim, "What happened to 'for better or worse'?" Therefore, I disagree with the strategy of putting a consortium claim in every case in which it may apply and have advised more than one of my clients to take it out before it gets to a jury. You need to think carefully about whether to include a loss of consortium claim. There are instances in which doing so can harm the jurors' perceptions of your and your clients' trustworthiness.

Moreover, the manner in which you handle loss of consortium at trial is also important to the credibility of the case as well as the likability of the plaintiffs. It often rubs jurors the wrong way to hear, for example, a wife testify about the extent to which she has been inconvenienced by her husband's illness. I recall a trial in Milwaukee in which a wife testified about how she needed to come back early from a tropical vacation because of her husband's medical problems. She had not been able to travel the way she wanted since the injury. As I was working for the defense in that matter, the testimony was music to my ears.

Loss of consortium is powerful when it illustrates the strength of the bond between spouses. This is best achieved by having each spouse talk about the other. To make an effective loss of consortium claim, have the wife tell about her concern for her injured husband, and have her husband tell how upset he is about being no longer able to contribute to the financial health of the household, putting the burden on his wife. That can be emotionally powerful. On the other hand, having a husband complain about the loss of "me time" or a wife express her upset about losing her tropical vacations? Not so powerful.

Loss of consortium is powerful when it illustrates the strength of the bond between spouses. This is best achieved by having each spouse talk about the other.

Loss of consortium is an important claim in those cases that warrant it. Not all cases do. In any event, you must handle it carefully. The rule of thumb is this: the more a spouse of an injured plaintiff talks about self, the less sympathy people will feel.

Questions to Ask Yourself

- Does the consortium plaintiff seem more concerned about his or her spouse or self?

- Is the loss of the consortium a true loss or an inconvenience?

- (*for plaintiffs*) Am I using the spouses' concerns for each other to tell the consortium story?

2.7   Defendants: Address Damages

In my practice as a jury consultant, I have seen many defense attorneys express concern that to a jury, defense counsel speaking about damages sounds like conceding liability. These perceptions likely come from the mouths of jurors themselves. I have heard jurors, on multiple occasions, proclaim that the defense must know that it did something wrong because it argued damages in its presentation. The important point to note here is that in every instance I have heard such a statement, it came from a juror who would have been plaintiff-oriented regardless. The utterance was something they used to support the belief already held, not the reason for the belief in the first place.

Other defense attorneys have shared their perspective that when they argue against injury-related damages, the jurors will see the defense as callous and dismissive of the plaintiff's injuries. Yes, that certainly can be the case if you present your damage argument in a manner that is callous and dismissive.

The fact of the matter is that there are ways to discuss a plaintiff's damages without agreeing that the defendant is liable for compensable damages, and you can do it in a manner that is neither callous nor dismissive.

Admittedly, there are pitfalls to arguing damages as a defendant if you do not carefully vet the arguments. On the other hand, the pitfalls of not doing so could be even more dangerous.

There are ways to discuss a plaintiff's damages without agreeing that the defendant is liable for compensable damages, and you can do it in a manner that is neither callous nor dismissive.

In a trucking accident case in New York City, a man's hand was severely injured when the side door of his van closed unexpectedly, shattering several bones. The injured plaintiff was suing for a large amount in damages, claiming that the door was pushed closed by the defendant's passing truck and that he was permanently injured. The plaintiff claimed that the injury left his hand so disfigured and him so depressed that he could no longer be intimate with his wife or play soccer with his son.

The defense conducted a mock trial for this case and vehemently argued against liability, stating that it would be impossible for the truck to get so close to the plaintiff's vehicle that it created an airflow pattern sufficient to cause the door to slam shut but not otherwise come into contact with any other part of the vehicle. In closing, the defense also argued damages head on.

In that damages discussion, counsel conceded the injury and recognized the plaintiff's pain. After those acknowledgements, counsel then argued, "But the plaintiff's damage claims are just one more example of how the plaintiff is overreaching in this case. Was his hand broken? Yes. Was it very painful? Yes. But is the plaintiff still able to have a fulfilling life despite having his hand broken? Yes." For the jurors in the exercise, this damage claim—in conjunction with other instances of overreaching—painted a portrait of a plaintiff who desired to collect money at the expense of reality. Therefore, the strategy did not only work in favor of the defendant for damages, but it also supported the liability case by underscoring the consistent theme that the plaintiff was untrustworthy.

Obviously, most injury cases involve much more than a broken hand. There are times when we are dealing with cases that involve terrible injuries that no one is exaggerating. In these cases, I advise against arguing the extent of the injury or the quality of care. It is rarely palatable to jurors to hear that a severely and permanently injured plaintiff can forego the best care or can go for something more cost effective. You can argue that there are care alternatives, but focusing on the costs of the care tends to be more effective than arguing the care itself, especially if the requested treatment seems reasonable at face value. And sometimes, even if not.

Of course, if the defense does make arguments suggesting suboptimal care, the door is open for plaintiff to come in full force to counter the argument—presenting the defense as callous and dismissive. Especially if the defendant is a corporation, plaintiff may question whether what the defense argues is "good enough" care for the plaintiff would be "good enough" for the company's CEO or her family.

In another trucking accident case in New York State, a woman suffered a head-on collision with a truck and was rendered a quadriplegic. In the mock trial exercise, the defense, as in the hand crush case, argued strongly against liability. In fact, there was evidence that this plaintiff fell asleep at the wheel and drifted into the oncoming path of the defendant's truck. When the defense counsel discussed damages, he agreed with all aspects of the plaintiff's injuries and with her life-care plan. It was what it was.

But by acknowledging the injuries and agreeing with the life-care plan, defense counsel was then free to spend the majority of her damages presentation on the economist's construction of the present value of the costs, which showed the jurors that the plaintiffs could receive the top-quality care with a dollar amount that was substantially less than what the plaintiff was claiming. The jurors told us that they were impressed that the defendant did not dismiss any aspect of the plaintiff's suffering, and were, therefore, more open to listening to the economic analysis. They weren't willing to take either side's economic forecast at face value, but felt the real cost of care was likely somewhere in the middle of the opposing numbers. The defense was effective at weighing the numbers down.

Jurors also agreed that the plaintiff caused the accident. The defense's damage argument did not mean they admitted liability. Instead, the reasonable damage argument presented the defense as a reasonable party, allowing jurors to stay open to what a corporation had to say, even when faced with horrendous injuries.

It is important not only to argue liability, but to mitigate damages without harming the rest of your case. There are ways you can do it, and you should do it.

For a defendant, there is always the possibility that jurors will find for plaintiff on liability. Therefore, it is important not only to argue liability, but to mitigate damages without harming the rest of your case. There are ways you can do it, and you should do it. With only one set of numbers for damages, the jurors have only one reference for calculating their damage award. When more than one set of damage models are provided, jurors will typically use both sets of numbers to determine what is fair. The research has shown that when you provide those alternative damage anchors, damages come down—especially when you do so with compassion and without conceding liability.

Questions to Ask Yourself

- Is there a dispute about the amount of damages in the case?

- (*for defendants*) Is there a risk of higher damages if the jurors' only damage numbers are presented by the plaintiffs?

- Are the defense's damages presented in a way that suggests suboptimal care for an injured plaintiff?

- Does the defense present alternative damages in a manner that attacks the character or integrity of the plaintiff or dismisses true suffering?

2.8   Plaintiffs: Assert Punitive Damages Wisely

I have to admit it is enticing for plaintiffs to put a punitive damage claim into cases. Punitive damages can make the case worth go sky high, theoretically. So why not put them into every case you can? There is a troubling truth for plaintiffs, and that truth is this: beware of punitive damage claims. In the wrong case and with the wrong strategy, they can actually hurt you.

Let's take the case of a difficult delivery of a baby in Minnesota. The plaintiff was having a difficult course during delivery, and there were signs that the baby was going into distress. The Caesarean-section team was on its way, but it would take some time for them to get there. The defendant OB-GYN doctor tried to use a vacuum device on the baby's head to get the baby out. It failed, but the doctor made several attempts before she was able to deliver the baby via Caesarean.

During the process of using the vacuum, the baby sustained an injury to the exterior of her head. The plaintiff sued, claiming that the child also sustained brain damage during the process. The plaintiff filed for punitive damages, accusing the doctor of battery. That's right, battery.

The severity of the accusations against this doctor who was clearly trying to get the baby delivered as quickly as possible was simply over the top. The plaintiff lost all credibility by going too far. Deliberations resulted in a verdict for the defense after less than an hour. Coffee break included.

Plaintiffs: beware of punitive damage claims. In the wrong case and with the wrong strategy, they can actually hurt you.

We can also examine the case involving the appliance fire that killed a young boy. The punitive damages claim was based on evidence that not only had other children died in similar fires started within the same make and model appliance, but more egregiously, the evidence from those other fires had been destroyed by the company. With that kind of corporate behavior, my clients, who represented the plaintiff, believed punitive damages should be a given. Of course they would be. But they weren't.

Despite some pretty devastating evidence against the company, jurors in our research exercise believed that the accusations underlying the punitive damage claim were unreasonably severe. Even in the face of the jury instructions, jurors translated the actions required to find punitive damages as "intent" to harm or an understanding that harm would certainly occur. Given that, the jurors seemed to characterize this company as most companies: "business is business." Specifically, the jurors did not believe that the company would purposely endanger customers or manufacture a common household product that it believed would kill a child. In their minds, it was just too severe an accusation.

In mock deliberations involving punitive damages, this is a conversation I hear time and time again. Despite strategies to define and reframe punitive damages, jurors instinctively connect punishment with intent. These observations are congruent with research on punitive damages conducted by Eisenberg et al. (1997), who compiled information from one year of jury verdicts from forty-five of the nations' most populous counties.[5] Results indicated that jurors are downright reluctant to award punitive damages, especially in product liability and medical malpractice cases.

Punitive damage claims are strongest when jurors see a clear pattern of intentional behavior and not just an isolated incident. I recall a crane accident case in which a company running a warehouse intentionally disabled a safety feature in their cranes that prevented the crane's hook from being pulled too high, which could cause the hook's cable to be cut. Company witnesses admitted in depositions that the safety feature was disabled because when the feature was triggered, it needed to be reset—a difficult and laborious process that resulted in lost productivity. As a result, a hook carrying a heavy load was pulled too high, the cable snapped, and the heavy load fell to the ground where an unsuspecting contractor was standing. Every one of the appalled jurors in the focus group wanted to award punitive damages. They saw the behavior as intentional. I was assisting the plaintiff, and we were ready to go full steam ahead at trial. Instead, the defense wisely paid one of the highest settlements in Philadelphia history at the time.

Despite strategies to define and reframe punitive damages, jurors instinctively connect punishment with intent.

In my experience, jurors struggle with punitive damages when the defendant is an individual (like in the case of the OB-GYN) and/or the defendant's behavior indicates neither intent nor a pattern of behavior.

Of greater concern for plaintiffs, I have seen the introduction of punitive damages cause jurors to become sympathetic to and even protective of the defendant. Just like in the OB-GYN's case, they asked, "if the plaintiff is way out of reach here, where else is she padding her story—where else is she unfairly accusing?"

The risk is clear: if jurors feel out of sync with the plaintiff's punitive damage arguments, that disconnect may overflow to other areas and pollute the entire plaintiff's case.

Once punitive damages are in the case, acknowledge the jurors' natural instincts when you clarify what punitive damages do and do not mean. For example, in the appliance fire case, plaintiff's counsel argued:

> By asking for punitive damages, are we saying that Company X has set out to harm children? Of course not. That would be absurd. Does it

---

5. T. Eisenberg, J. Goerdt, B. Ostrom, D. Rottman & M. T. Wells, *The Predictability of Punitive Damages*, 26 THE JOURNAL OF LEGAL STUDIES 623 (1997).

mean, though, that Company X let a product go out into the community that it knew had a defect? Yes. That it knew this kind of accident could happen? Yes. That it knew the kinds of horrific injuries these accidents cause to kids? Yes.

Ladies and gentlemen, we are not saying that Company X wants to hurt little children. What we are saying is that knowing the risk, it did nothing to protect children. We submit to you that placing the risk into the community while closing its eyes and crossing its fingers meets the definition of reckless indifference and so meets the standard for punitive damages the judge will provide you.

Because of the evidence of bad—i.e., beyond what the jurors would normally expect—corporate behavior in this case, the jurors did not hold it against the plaintiff for asserting punitive damages. So, in this instance, the claim didn't harm plaintiff's case in the way the severe accusations did in the case of the doctor using the vacuum device during delivery. But it is noteworthy that jurors were still reluctant to award punitive damages. So they didn't. They had made their point in a headline-making compensatory award.

Questions to Ask Yourself

- How likely is it that punitive damages will be awarded in this case?

- Is the defendant an individual or a corporation?

- Were the defendant's actions part of a larger pattern of behavior or a one-time occurrence?

- Will jurors see the defendant's conduct as intentional?

- (*for plaintiffs*) Will my punitive damage argument detract from my liability case by reaching too far?

2.9 Look at Your Verdict Form—Again

The word choice of a verdict form in jury trials is critical. Jurors can easily misinterpret a question that can be interpreted in multiple ways to the detriment of your case.

As Owen Fiss writes in "Objectivity and Interpretation":

> Interpretation, whether it be in the law or literary domain, is neither wholly discretionary nor a wholly mechanical activity. It is a dynamic interaction between reader and text, and meaning the product of that interaction. It is an activity that affords a proper recognition of both the subjective and objective dimensions of human experience.[6]

What Fiss asserts is as true at trial as it is in literature. Take, for example, a Minneapolis trial involving facial plastic surgery. The plaintiff, a man in his sixties, received a facelift from his plastic surgeon. Aesthetically, the results of the surgery were good. The issue was that the plaintiff complained of facial pain, although no physiological reason could be found for his pain. The plaintiff claimed the surgeon was negligent. His experts determined that a nerve must have been cut during the procedure because that was the only feasible explanation for the pain. The plaintiff also claimed that the surgeon failed to get the plaintiff's informed consent. The plaintiff asserted that he was unaware that permanent pain was a risk of the surgery and that if he had been told that was the case, he would not have had the procedure done.

In the end, the jury found that the doctor was not negligent and that he met the standard of care regarding the manner in which he conducted the surgery. They did, however, find for the plaintiff on the issue of informed consent. After the trial, we interviewed members of the jury to get a sense of how they came to their verdict. The panel members told us that they felt a higher standard of informed consent should apply to an elective procedure like plastic surgery than to a surgery necessary to alleviate a health condition. They applied this higher standard in their interpretation. Because the jurors had such negative perceptions of plastic surgery in general, they felt that plastic surgeons should go so far as to try and talk their patients out of the procedures. That clearly was not done in this case.

Because the jurors found that the defendant did not solicit adequate informed consent for the procedure, the jurors considered the causation verdict question as it appeared on the verdict form—whether a "reasonable person" would have refused the surgery had more information been given. They answered "yes."

As we learned in the post-verdict interviews, the jurors actually felt that the plaintiff himself would have had the surgery regardless of any risk communicated. But, they

---

6. Owen Fiss, *Objectivity and Interpretation*, 34 STAN. L. REV. 739 (1982).

explained, that wasn't the question on the verdict form. The question was whether a "reasonable person" would have refused. This was a critical distinction. In fact, jurors found that the plaintiff was an unreasonable person in his quest for the fountain of youth. However, because the question asked about a "reasonable person," what the perceived unreasonable plaintiff would have done with the additional information was irrelevant to the answer.

This jury, comprised of all females except for one male, put the standard of being "reasonable" on that one male juror. That is, they decided that their male counterpart was a reasonable person, and they asked him if he would have had the surgery. His answer was "no." He, a male in his twenties, personally would not have had a facelift. He found getting a facelift unreasonable, in general, let alone considering the potential complications. Therefore, because of the way the jurors chose to interpret the causation question, the lone male juror's answer stuck, and the jury found for the plaintiff. When it came to damages, the jurors simply reimbursed the plaintiff for the cost of the surgery.

In 1995, University of Pittsburgh scholar, Douglas Hartman, studied how individuals made connections as they interpreted the meaning of texts.[7] In this study, he found that his subjects made two kinds of intertextual links to develop meaning. The first connected ideas, events, and people. The second connected social, cultural, political, and historical contexts.

This study is particularly interesting when you consider how jurors link social and cultural context when interpreting the language on a verdict form. The social and cultural context of the courtroom is one that jurors often struggle with as they try to marry the rules and rituals of our litigation system with their perception of what is "right."

I have seen several cases in which verdicts are won or lost on the way the question on a verdict form is worded. Because they are in unfamiliar legal territory, jurors tend to look at the semantics of questions and interpret them quite literally.

In the plastic surgery case, the jurors linked the importance of following the law in its literal form to how they interpreted the verdict questions in their literal form. The jurors believed that the social and cultural context of the courtroom required them to answer what was literally on the page in front of them, even if it didn't seem logical. These jurors struggled to reconcile their desire to comport with the court's expectations, their feeling that the plaintiff did not deserve to be rewarded, and their feelings against plastic surgery. Even though it may not have made intuitive sense

---

7. Douglas K. Hartman, *Eight Readers Reading: The Intertextual Links of Proficient Readers Reading Multiple Passages*, 30 Reading Research Quarterly 520 (1995).

to them, the jurors acted in accordance with what they believed to be the values of the courtroom—but they restored equilibrium and a feeling of fairness by awarding nominal damages.

I have seen several cases in which verdicts are won or lost on the way the question on a verdict form is worded. Because they are in unfamiliar legal territory, jurors tend to look at the semantics of questions and interpret them quite literally. Therefore, it is critical that you closely examine the wording on the verdict form, not just for legal sense, but for the manner in which it can be misinterpreted. Where you can argue for semantic change, argue for it. Regardless of the words on the verdict form, walk the jurors carefully through it in closings. Provide the roadmap of issues they should consider when answering each question. Without that direction, in the foreign land of litigation, jurors are more apt to get lost.

Questions to Ask Yourself

- What does the literal language of the verdict form ask for?

- How can that language be misinterpreted?

- Do I have enough distance or objectivity to determine that or do I need to get an outside opinion?

- How can I change the language so it's clearer?

- How am I addressing what the verdict form questions mean and how they connect to the evidence in my presentation to the jurors?

2.10 Be Wary of Online Focus Groups

It's all the rage. It is pretty darn cool, and it is much less expensive than the old, archaic way of doing things: online mock trials. Some technology now even has avatars of the mock jurors sitting around a discussion table talking about your case. There are myriad new and interesting ways to get juror feedback about a case without even leaving the comforts of your office.

Sorry to say, I am not yet convinced.

I am open to having my mind changed. Really, I am. But I haven't heard anything yet that will make me think that conducting a mock trial with a group of people in different rooms and different houses and different towns is a good idea. I am uncomfortable relying on the feedback of people you can't see, who you can't be sure are really there and paying attention or instead getting a snack, or checking their email, or playing Sudoku, or letting their teenaged son take their place because they need to run to the grocery store. Call me old-fashioned.

My concerns about online honesty are warranted, and similar concerns have been studied in the field of business. Research has been conducted on the subject of deception in business using online systems versus traditional methods of communication. Jeanne Logsdon and Karen Patterson (2009) found a greater likelihood that people will deceive through online communications in business dealings.[8] In their work, Logsdon and Patterson identify how the medium of communication influences the probability of deception. I am confident that the phenomenon extends well beyond their research subject matter.

Given that, let's say you can get those identity concerns under control and there are ways to make sure that the person providing the feedback is actually there and paying attention. Sorry, still not convinced.

Outright deception aside, this approach abrogates two important aspects of communication—the "central message" of words being said and the "peripheral message" of everything that happens around the words such as nonverbal communication, tone, and personal dynamics. Is the person raising his or her voice? Has she crossed her arms and pushed back from the table? Is he watching the presentations intently or snoring? How are people reacting to one another across the table in deliberations? How are they trying to convince one another of their opposing positions in the case? The human dynamic is an enormous part of the courtroom, not only for witnesses and their communications, but for jurors as well.

Researchers David Jonassen and Hyug Kwon performed a study on the nature of group dynamics in different communicative contexts and reported their results in their 2001 article "Communication Patterns in Computer-Mediated versus Face-to-

---

8. Jeanne M. Logsdon & Karen D. W. Patterson, *Deception in Business Networks: Is It Easier to Lie Online?*, 90 JOURNAL OF BUSINESS ETHICS 537 (2009).

Face Group Problem Solving."[9] They found that group dynamics change depending on the medium of communication. Problem-solving cooperation becomes more personal when people meet face-to-face rather than communicate online. Of course it does.

While we do our best to capture a high level idea of how humans react in a human way to a case, I think these important dynamics are truncated quite enough in the context of a traditional mock trial in which we present the case without live witnesses (usually) and in a much shorter period of time. It is one thing to ask someone to rate their anger toward a party on a scale from 0 to 10 and quite another to see how people speak with or without emotion about their feelings toward that party and discover the relevant experiences that impact those feelings.

Why would we want to control the discussion so much that we lose the ability to observe the jurors engaging in a real debate across a table? What happened to the value of seeing people interact in the same manner jurors will at trial?

So I ask, what are we gaining from taking so much of the human element out of these exercises by conducting them online with a group of folks who haven't met or seen each other? Will we be able to understand how participants are actually reacting? Why are we erasing the context of the jurors' reactions to each other's nonverbal communications? Why would we want to control the discussion so much that we lose the ability to observe the jurors engaging in a real debate across a table? What happened to the value of seeing people interact in the same manner jurors will at trial?

Not every case warrants a live mock trial or focus group, but I believe that we have to consider what constitutes useful information from a reliable source. Call me "old school," but I believe that currently, online focus groups lose too much of what is real about people's interaction and the way they will behave and react in the courtroom. As a result, I still hesitate to use it as a resource to make decisions about important cases. I am ready and willing to be convinced otherwise. It just hasn't happened yet.

---

9. David H. Jonassen & Hyug Kwon, *Communication Patterns in Computer-Mediated versus Face-to-Face Group Problem Solving*, 49 Educational Technology Research and Development 35 (2001).

Questions to Ask Yourself

- Does my case really need a focus group?

- What do I hope to get from my focus group?

- Is my focus group panel representative of the likely jurors in my venue?

- Do I know for certain that my participants are who they say they are?

- Am I risking being misled by a non-representative panel?

- Is there another, more reliable way to get an outside perspective while keeping the budget where I need it to be?

2.11 Transactional Attorneys: Consider the Jury

In the early 2010s, I was a part of a panel at the American Bar Association's Forum on Franchising in San Diego, California. As a part of the presentation, the panel members and I used Real Time Technology™ to ask the 500-member audience multiple-choice questions. With the technology, the audience could answer the questions electronically using a device we provided. We immediately could both see and show the audience members how they answered each question.

One of the first questions we asked was whether the audience agreed or disagreed with the statement: "Jury issues have nothing to do with my practice." Most of the audience, comprised of a mixture of litigators, corporate counsel, and transactional attorneys, disagreed.

However, when we broke down the responses to determine how they differed according to the kinds of law the audience members practiced, the transactional attorneys stood separate and apart from the rest. Over 70 percent of transactional attorneys agreed that jury issues have nothing to do with their practice. Was I surprised? No. Did I have something to say about it? Absolutely.

The fact of the matter is that in many commercial cases, attorneys who believe their practice need not consider juries are the very people whose work is being interpreted and considered by juries. These attorneys write the contracts that jurors will later interpret, develop the processes that jurors may later evaluate, conduct the due diligence that jurors will examine, approve the messages in the product manuals jurors review . . . shall I continue?

Contracts written in language that the everyday person finds confusing lead jurors to give the benefit of the doubt to the side of the case that did not write them. Just like manuals that do not contain the warnings recommended by industry standards will cause jurors to question the safety practices of the entire company. In essence, the failure to consider how transactional issues may later be interpreted by laypeople has led to many a lawsuit, and unfortunately, many a bad trial result.

The walls erected between the transactional and litigation professionals within an organization should, needless to say, be replaced with open lines of communication. An ounce of prevention is worth a pound of cure. That prevention is often within the jurisdiction of the transactional attorney, for whom jury issues and layperson interpretation are farthest from her mind. However, the transactional attorney should consider these issues more closely as she writes contracts and reviews.

In essence, the failure to consider how transactional issues may later be interpreted by laypeople has led to many a lawsuit, and unfortunately, many a bad trial result.

Remember, just because an attorney does not see jurors in her practice doesn't mean that a jury will not be seeing that attorney's work at trial.

Questions to Ask Yourself

- Do I think jury issues have nothing to do with my practice?

- Will the litigators who deal with lawsuits regarding the contracts and manuals I write agree with me?

- Will the language of the legal documents I write be confusing to the average person?

- How can transactional and litigation attorneys better communicate in my field to be proactive?

PART THREE

DESELECTING JURIES

3.1 Know Your Biases

How aware are we of our own unconscious biases? Most people, the research indicates, are not aware at all. That is why they are unconscious. The truth is that all of us have them. No exceptions.

So how do we become aware of our own biases? Luckily, there is a test specifically designed to evaluate just that. It is called Harvard's Implicit Association Test. Take it. You will probably learn something about yourself that you didn't really want to know. But if you are a trial lawyer, or anyone who interacts with people on a regular basis, understanding your own biases is vital.

A team of social psychologists led by Dr. Anthony Greenwald developed the Implicit Association Test in 1998 to tap into attitudes and associations we hold that are underneath our consciousness.[1] The test involves pairing words or images with words. For example, if you take the test, you may see the word "Black" on the top left-hand corner of your screen and "White" on the right. In the middle of the screen you would see a word, such as a first name, that is typically associated with either the categories of "Black" or "White." If you associate the word in the middle as more associated with "Black," you would press a left hand key. You'd press a right hand key if you associate the word with "White."

In another phase of the test, the task would be the same, but the words on the top right and left would be opposing attributes like "Pleasant" or "Unpleasant." Then you would be asked to pair a word that appeared in the middle as either "Pleasant" or "Unpleasant."

Finally, the tasks would be combined. So you may see the words "Black/Pleasant" in the top left-hand corner and "White/Unpleasant" in the top right-hand. Again, based on a name or word in the middle, you would be asked to press the left-hand

---

1. Anthony G. Greenwald, D. E. McGhee & J. K. L Schwartz, *Measuring Individual Differences in Implicit Cognition: The Implicit Association Test*, 74 JOURNAL OF PERSONALITY AND SOCIAL PSYCHOLOGY 1464 (1998).

key if the name or word belongs to the "Black/Pleasant" category or the right-hand key if it belongs to the "White/Unpleasant" category.

The tasks are repeated using varying positions and combinations of words, names, and attributes. The theory is that when the word pairings are compatible with implicit associations or beliefs, the task is easier. It takes less time to press the appropriate button. When the pairings are not compatible, it takes more time to make the connection. The study has shown, since its inception in 1998 and over thousands of participants, that people are able to categorize more quickly when "White" and "Pleasant" are paired together than when "Black" and "Pleasant" are paired, indicating more positive associations with the concept of "White." Consistently. The findings apply to test takers of all races.

How do we become aware of our own biases? Luckily, there is a test specifically designed to evaluate just that. It is called Harvard's Implicit Association Test. Take it. You will probably learn something about yourself that you didn't really want to know. But if you are a trial lawyer, or anyone who interacts with people on a regular basis, understanding your own biases is vital.

The Implicit Association Test has been most widely cited in examining associations we make toward people of different races, but has been used in other fields as well, such as consumer decision-making, where we can more easily link associations with decisions. In 2004, the test's creator, Anthony Greenwald and fellow researchers had subjects take the test to see what their underlying opinions were of different brands of yogurt, restaurants, and soft drinks.[2] They found, not surprisingly, that the unconscious associations elicited in the test predicted the research participants' brand preference, brand recognition, and product usage.

In an alarming application of this phenomenon to the courtroom, John Irwin and Daniel Real discovered that the same implicit bias impacts judicial decision-making in the very same manner.[3] They found that judges' underlying opinions of demographic groups were significantly associated with their findings of criminal defendants' guilt or innocence.

The fact of the matter is that biases, whether we are aware of them or not, guide our behaviors, possibly in contrast to other more rational basis of those decisions. Biases may compel some people to hire or not hire a person, to cross to the other side of the street at a particular person's approach, or, of course, to strike a potential juror.

---

2. D. Maison, Anthony G. Greenwald & R. H. Bruin, *Predictive Validity of the Implicit Association Test in Studies of Brands, Consumer Attitudes and Behavior*, 14 Journal of Consumer Psychology 404 (2004).
3. John F. Irwin & Daniel L. Real, *Unconscious Influences on Judicial Decision-Making: The Illusion of Objectivity*, 43 McGeorge L. Rev. 1 (2010).

National Institute for Trial Advocacy

Looking deeper into how bias comes about, one clear finding is that its development starts very early in childhood. Children as young as three years old begin to identify themselves with social categories and express preferences for those categories.[4] Negative intergroup attitudes emerge between ages four and five.[5] Think of the gender-dividing epidemic of "cooties" in elementary school. What is more disturbing, although not surprising, is that children from socially disadvantaged groups are more likely to show preference for groups perceived to be more valued by the mainstream as opposed to their own demographic group.[6]

The body of research suggests that because biases are developed extremely early in life and become so well imbedded into our subconscious by adulthood, we are hardly aware of them. This is an important part of what can make bias so damaging in so many ways.

In 2006, Justin Levinson conducted some pretty astounding research on racial bias and its relationship to misremembering facts.[7] In his study, he had participant groups read case vignettes about either a fight or employment termination. The groups read the same story, but the race of the characters involved were varied for different groups. When the participants were asked to recall the story facts, Levinson found that facts were significantly misremembered in a racially biased manner. Even more interesting, he found this phenomenon not only when participants were asked to remember facts individually, but also in group deliberations, where the participants collectively were also unlikely to resolve the issue.

Levinson used his research to argue that both judges and jurors may unknowingly propagate racism through their legal decisions because they misremember case facts in implicitly biased ways. This, in combination with John Irwin and Daniel Real's findings about the influence of bias on judicial decisions, makes it clear that implicit bias always has a presence and impact in the courtroom.

While most of the considerations of implicit bias have been applied to verdict-related decision-making, it begs the question of what other implications can be ascribed to this phenomenon. If judges and juries have been empirically found to make decisions affected by bias, it only makes sense that attorneys are also affected by their own implicit associations in voir dire.

---

4. F. E. Aboud & M. Amato, *Developmental and Socialization Influences on Intergroup Bias*, BLACKWELL HANDBOOK OF SOCIAL PSYCHOLOGY: INTERGROUP PROCESSES 65–85 (2001).

5. Rebecca S. Bigler, *The Role of Classification Skill in Moderating Environmental Effects on Children's Gender Stereotyping: A Study of the Functional Use of Gender in the Classroom*, 66 CHILD DEVELOPMENT 1072 (1995).

6. Nilanjana Dasgupta, *Implicit In-Group Favoritism, Out-Group Favoritism, and Their Behavioral Manifestations*, 17 SOCIAL JUSTICE RESEARCH 143 (2004).

7. Justin D. Levinson, *Forgotten Racial Equality: Implicit Bias, Decision-Making, and Misremembering*, 57 DUKE L.J. 345 (2007).

We know now that we all have biases and that some of us hold biases against our own demographic group, but what does it all mean in the jury context? In their article, "Race and Jury Selection," Samuel Sommers and Michael Norton discuss how stereotypes are likely to affect judgments made on limited information, under cognitive overload, and under time pressure.[8] That sounds like jury selection to me. They also highlighted the social implications of attorney tendencies to strike people based on race, regardless of the Supreme Court's 1986 *Batson v. Kentucky* decision, which outlawed the practice. They expressed concern about the social message that people of certain races are poor decision-makers.

The article by Sommers and Norton got me thinking, though, not just about the social implications related to making decisions based on race, but the strategic implications as well. Specifically, do biases lead trial teams to make the wrong juror-striking choices?

In regard to making the wrong decisions by focusing solely on demographic variables such as race, we may consider some research on perpetrator profiling in the field of national security. William Press looked into the controversial subject of profiling for additional security screening at airports and the like based on nationality or ethnicity. He found that "strong profiling," or screening in proportion to malfeasance statistics by ethnicity or nationality, is no more efficient in finding bad actors than uniform random sampling of the entire population. The issue, he found, was that there was a greater and repeated attention paid toward innocent individuals within a particular ethnic group or nationality while people that fell outside of that ethnic group were sampled too infrequently.[9]

As in national security, focusing too strongly on ethnicity in jury selection and failing to account for the possibility that the most dangerous juror may be outside your expected demographic category can be detrimental to your case.

The juror profiling research I have conducted has revealed, time and time again, that demographic variables such as race and gender typically are not the most salient predictors of verdict orientation—attitudes and experiences relevant to the case and its subject matter are. On the other hand, time and time again, I am asked by litigators which race and gender variable they should focus on in jury selection. I observe trial teams make visceral judgments based on demographic characteristics, relying on what they can easily see and their gut reaction to a potential juror. As the research has told us, those gut reactions may just come from an unconscious bias or stereotype.

---

8. Samuel S. Sommers & Michael I. Norton, *Race and Jury Selection: Psychological Perspectives on the Preemptory Challenge Debate*, 63 AMERICAN PSYCHOLOGIST 527 (2008).
9. William Press, *Strong Profiling Is Not Mathematically Optimal for Discovering Rare Malfeasors*, 106 PROCEEDINGS OF THE NATIONAL ACADEMY OF SCIENCES OF THE UNITED STATES OF AMERICA 1716 (2009).

The next time you are in jury selection, ask yourself this question before you make a strike: "Am I making this strike because this juror is likely biased against my client or because I am likely biased against this juror?"

I remember a jury selection in Chicago. Before voir dire began, an attorney told me he once had one Hispanic male on a prior jury who found against his client. He then proclaimed that he would never allow another Hispanic male on a jury again. In racially diverse Cook County, that attorney was using one demographic characteristic to make his striking decisions. Every single trial. Well, except the one with which I was assisting.

So take the Implicit Association Test, and the next time you are in jury selection, ask yourself this question before you make a strike: "Am I making this strike because this juror is likely biased against my client or because I am likely biased against this juror?"

Questions to Ask Yourself

- Where do I hold my biases?

- How do my biases impact the decisions I make in jury selection?

- Am I focused primarily on demographic variables in making my strikes?

- Am I doing my client a disservice by focusing on demographics in jury selection?

3.2   Think Beyond a Universal Jury Profile

In the field of the psychology of risk and uncertainty, researchers William Samuelson and Richard Zeckhauser conducted a social experiment and found that people tend to hold a strong bias toward maintaining the status quo.[10] In their research, they presented their subjects with real decision-making tasks, such as selecting health plans or investments or retirement programs. The subjects were split into groups with one of two conditions.

In the first condition (Group 1) of the research, subjects received the following explanation of a decision (considered the neutral version that was presented to the control group):

> You are a serious reader of financial pages, but until recently have had few funds to invest. That is when you inherited a large sum of money from your great uncle. You are considering different portfolios.

Participants in the second research condition (Group 2) received this alternative explanation of the decision (considered the status quo version that was presented to the experimental group):

> You are a serious reader of the financial pages, but until recently have had few funds to invest. That is when you inherited a portfolio of cash and securities from your great uncle. A significant portion of this portfolio is invested in moderate-risk Company A. You are deliberating whether to leave the portfolio intact or to change it by investing in other securities. (The tax and broker commission consequences of any change are insignificant).

The choices for different investment options were identical for both groups. The only variable at issue was whether the subject was presented with deciding on a new plan or changing a plan already in place.

What the experimenters found was that the respondents who were given the version of the questionnaire in which they would need to change an already existing plan disproportionately made decisions that maintained the established decision instead of making a change. Using different decision scenarios, they found that this bias toward maintaining previously made decisions is pervasive, regardless of what kind of decision is being made.[11] People simply feel more comfortable maintaining the status quo.

In the political arena, the authors purport that this bias toward the status quo is one of the reasons why an incumbent candidate tends to have a significant advantage over a newcomer. We tend to go with what we think we know.

---

10. William Samuelson & Richard Zeckhauser, *Status Quo Bias in Decision-Making*, 1 JOURNAL OF RISK AND UNCERTAINTY 7 (1988).

11. *Id.*

When it comes to simple, daily decision tasks like what we eat for breakfast or what shampoo to buy, the status quo, also known as habit, makes our lives easier. We don't have to think deeply about each and every action. It becomes ingrained. We are wired this way because it conserves our mental energy. The problem arises when this same system that conserves our mental energy in the menial tasks of daily life creep into the decisions we make at a higher level. It affects the decisions that we should examine more critically—decisions such as what health or retirement plan to employ, as were tested in the experiment cited above, or decisions regarding what characteristics of jurors you should look for when making striking decisions in jury selection.

While litigators focus on this kind of phenomenon in jurors, acknowledging that jurors will tend to believe stories that comport with the opinions that they already hold, we also need to examine closely how psychological principles such as Samuelson and Zeckhauser's "status quo bias" affects how you make decisions about jury selection and trial strategies in general.

Samuelson and Zeckhauser surmise, based on the results of their research, that "[t]he individual may retain the status quo out of convenience, habit or inertia, policy (company or government) or custom, because of fear or innate conservatism, or through simple rationalization."[12] Whatever the reason, be aware of simply defaulting to the status quo when you choose trial strategies and consider whether you do your client a disservice by choosing so.

So what does the comfort of the status quo have to do with jury selection? It relates to the fact that I see so many attorneys strike based on the same juror profile in every jury selection. Plaintiffs strike white, educated, professional males, whereas defendants strike black women of low socio-economic status. Depending on the case, using this striking strategy can be ill-advised for both sides.

Sticking with the status quo and one universal profile for all cases can lead you to strike the wrong jurors if you aren't careful.

Maybe attorneys focus on the same juror characteristics in every trial because of bad past experiences with people of a demographic group. This was the issue for the attorney in Chicago, who struck all Hispanic male jurors on all trials because of one Hispanic male juror who, once upon a time, didn't like his case. Maybe attorneys stick with one profile because they think that for a certain *type* of case—be it products liability, trucking, or contracts—the juror profile stays the same within that case category regardless of the idiosyncrasies of the different case stories. Maybe attorneys are being lulled into the comfort of the status quo.

---

12. *Id.* at 10.

Sticking with the status quo and one universal profile for all cases can lead you to strike the wrong jurors if you aren't careful.

Avoiding the assumption of a standard profile was a game-changing issue in a New Jersey patent matter that involved the manufacturing process for animal medication. I'll call it the "cute and fluffy bunny" medication. I was working for the defense, and the court had already determined that my client's process infringed. The trial was for damages only. There were millions of dollars at stake.

So what was the juror profile for this case? Because the defendant already had been found to have infringed, we wanted the conservative, corporate-minded person who would understand our perspective on an intellectual level, right? We wanted to avoid emotional jurors who would see us the badly behaving company that got caught red handed, right? Wrong.

There was another aspect to this story that turned the profile in this case upside down. Although the process by which the defendant made the medication was found to have infringed, the actual medication and its effects on the animals were quite different. The defendant's medication was proven to be much better for the health of the cute and fluffy bunnies. In fact, the evidence was that the plaintiff's medication, with its patented process, made the cute and fluffy bunnies sick . . . or even killed them.

So what happened? According to our mock trial research and the profiling statistics we conducted with the data, jurors who were more favorable to the defense were actually those who are traditionally seen as plaintiff-oriented. They did not view this case from a business perspective. They viewed it from a cute and fluffy bunny perspective. They did not like the fact that the plaintiff was trying to stop the defendant from making the better medication.

When we got to court, it was clear that the plaintiff hadn't conducted the profiling research we had and believed that the traditional juror profile applied to the case. Consequently, both sides were striking the same profile of people—those seen as favorable to defendants in the "traditional" profile. We were left with a jury full of cute and fluffy bunny loving folks. Verdict: the exact royalty recommended by the defense.

Questions to Ask Yourself

- Do I assume the same juror profile for all of my jury trials?

- Have I been lulled into staying with the status quo?

- How is my current case different from my prior cases?

- How may the idiosyncrasies of this case affect the profile of my worst juror?

3.3 Recognize Leaders

One persuasive person can make all the difference. That is why, in jury selection, I not only focus on those characteristics that will make jurors biased against my client, but also those that give a person the kind of charisma that will make her a persuasive thought leader in deliberations.

Leadership is a topic that has been studied and discussed extensively in business journals and academic research. In 2010, for example, de Vries, Bakker-Pieper, and Oostenveld conducted a study that evaluated different leadership styles. In their research, they surveyed 279 employees of a governmental organization. They then categorized their leadership findings into six communication styles: verbal aggressiveness, expressiveness, preciseness, assuredness, supportiveness, and argumentativeness.[13]

In the jury context, one of the main goals of voir dire is to get a sense of who the leaders may be on a panel. Who will be the foreperson, and what kind of impact will that person have on the other members of the panel? In that and other contexts, we often perceive leaders as those who are outwardly talkative, dynamic, and forceful with their opinions. In other words, we associate leaders as those who act in line with de Vries et al.'s verbal aggressiveness and argumentativeness. In doing so, we focus on the wrong characteristics. What these scholars found is that the strongest leaders are not always the loudest—other qualities abound that make someone the kind of person others will actually want to follow.

The research suggested that preciseness is the characteristic that most clearly indicates perceived leader performance and satisfaction with the leader, and this is above and beyond other leadership style variables. It isn't about being loud. It is about being clear. Precision makes it easy for others to know what to do and where to go. It is the comfort of organization and clarity as opposed to leadership by volume, which can feel like chaos.

In Malcolm Gladwell's book, *The Tipping Point*,[14] he discusses the precision type leaders and their power to bring other people to act, to adopt an idea or to purchase a product. He calls them "salesmen." In your jury, these are the panel members that sell a case idea or concept in such an effective manner that the other jurors will follow. Having a person like this on your jury can be like having a jury of one person. You convince her, she will convince everyone else with precision. If she is against you, she will turn everyone else against you. All I have to say is that if voir dire reveals someone who appears to have that kind of strong leadership potential, you need to be pretty darn confident she is going to be on your side to keep her on

---

13. Reinout E. de Vries, Angelique Bakker-Pieper & Wyneke Oostenveld, *Leadership = Communication? The Relations of Leaders' Communication Styles with Leadership Styles, Knowledge Sharing and Leadership Outcomes*, 25 JOURNAL OF BUSINESS AND PSYCHOLOGY 367 (2010).
14. MALCOLM GLADWELL, THE TIPPING POINT: HOW LITTLE THINGS CAN MAKE A BIG DIFFERENCE (2000).

the jury. For me, if I am not confident about which side she will support, she will be my number one strike (or, more likely, my final strike if I decide to play chicken with opposing counsel, hoping they strike her first).

A Pennsylvania focus group in which one of these powerful salesmen participated comes to mind. The case at issue involved an emotionally charged story about an injury to a child. Deliberations were heavy with debate. As the other panel members argued, the salesman did not jump out of the box, yelling his opinions. He was too effective for that. Instead, he sat. He watched. He listened. He didn't say a word. He didn't volunteer to be the foreperson. Once the rest of the jurors became exhausted and frustrated with one another, he spoke—not only from his own perspective, but using what he had gained from the other jurors' opinions. He spoke with a certain grace and sophistication that drew people in. He didn't say much, but after he did, no other juror voiced an opinion independent from his interpretation. The salesman was selling, and the rest of the jurors were buying.

When assessing leadership, you must ask not only if there is a person who has the confidence and assertiveness to lead. You also must consider whether that person has the kind of charisma that will make others want to follow and the precise clarity so they can follow.

At the end of their deliberation, I sat down and discussed the case with the group, actively trying to get opinions from the other jurors. They repeatedly referred back to what the salesman had said, repeating his words and starting sentences with "Well, I just agree with Bob" or "As Bob said . . . ."

Therefore, when assessing leadership, you must ask not only if there is a person who has the confidence and assertiveness to lead. You also must consider whether that person has the kind of charisma that will make others want to follow and the precise clarity so they can follow.

The good news is that a powerful salesman will more likely than not make herself known in jury selection if given a chance. She will speak with confidence in voir dire and happily provide opinion with clarity and precision. For this reason, if the court process allows, ask questions that are open-ended. Getting a sense of communication styles by letting jurors speak freely will give you a better picture of confidence, charisma, and eloquence—the telltale signs of a salesman. Getting just the facts in voir dire may help you identify basic characteristics in your juror profile, but hearing the manner in which someone speaks lets you know more about the interpersonal style or skills of that person.

After all, the power of one can make all the difference.

Questions to Ask Yourself

- How am I defining what makes a leader?

- Am I focusing on how outspoken a juror is or how effective?

- Does the voir dire system of my trial allow me to assess jurors' communication styles?

3.4   Ask the Questions You Need to Ask

Imagine that I have asked you to take part in a research study in which I have you and other respondents read a list of words. Depending on which testing group you happen to be in, the words you receive are either considered negative:

- war;

- damage;

- harm;

- gray;

- winter;

or positive:

- rainbow;

- beach;

- play;

- vacation;

- fun.

Assume that after reading those words, you were asked to look at faces with neutral expressions and project emotions onto those faces. Research in the field of social psychology suggests that if you read negative words before viewing the pictures, you would ascribe negative emotions such as "sadness" or "anger" to the neutral faces. If you had read positive words, you would be more likely to ascribe more positive emotions like "thoughtful" or "peaceful" to those same faces.[15] What is in your mind has more of an impact on what you see than what is actually there. And the research suggests that external cues are able to shape and manipulate what is in your mind.

In the field of social psychology, this phenomenon is called "priming," and it has caused more than a little bit of controversy. Are people really led down the primrose path that easily?

Perhaps the most widely recognized research on priming was conducted by psychologist John Bargh and his co-authors, Mark Chen and Lara Burrows.[16] In this research, undergraduates were asked to rearrange lists of words like "bingo" and "Florida," "knits" and "wrinkles," "bitter" and "alone" into sensible sentences.

---

15. Robert J. Oxoby & Hugh Finnigan, *Developing Heuristic-Based Quality Judgments: Blocking in Consumer Choice*, 24 Psychology and Marketing 295 (2007).

16. John A. Bargh, Mark Chen & Lara Burrows, *Automaticity of Social Behavior: Direct Effects of Trait Construct and Stereotype Activation on Action*, 71 Journal of Personality and Social Psychology 230 (1996).

The students thought that the experiment was about language ability. In reality, the content of the words was designed to prime the student to think of elderly people. In the experiment, when the student left the testing office, one of the experimenters was in the hallway with a hidden stopwatch, timing how long it took the student to walk a measured distance down the hall. The length of time to walk this distance was what was actually being tested.

What Bargh and his colleagues found was that students primed with information to make them think of the elderly walked more slowly than students in a control group who were exposed to words not associated with the elderly. In other words, the researchers concluded that because the participants were exposed to words representing "old," they acted old. The same authors also conducted similar experiments that found that when primed with words that were considered cues for "rudeness," their respondents were more apt to interrupt a staged conversation immediately after constructing the sentences.

Since that study was published in the Journal of Personality and Social Psychology in 1996, it has been cited more than 2,000 times and criticized almost as strongly. Its reliability has been questioned because other researchers have had difficulty replicating the findings. This begs the question of whether people are really that prone to suggestion. Is there actually some reality to George Lucas's "Jedi Mind Tricks" in his *Star Wars* films?

Are you actually tainting your jury pool by asking their perceptions of relevant issues before you give them a case story? Some attorneys and jury researchers believe that as a result of research like the studies cited above, you are. I disagree.

If we are to believe people are that easily primed, what kinds of suggestions are you making when you ask voir dire questions at trial or in a mock jury exercise? Are you actually tainting your jury pool by asking their perceptions of relevant issues before you give them a case story? Some attorneys and jury researchers believe that as a result of research like the studies cited above, you are.

I disagree.

First of all, controversy about replicability notwithstanding, most of these research findings are about the influence of flash stimuli. They are about a set of words and a flash of a face or an immediate behavioral response. They are about the impulsive response. Not the thoughtful one. Trials and mock jury exercises subject people to hours or days of information. The impact of information throughout a trial will be vastly more powerful than any prior suggestion by a voir dire question.

Secondly, in the research cited above, the stimuli provided were clearly biased toward one end of the emotional spectrum and a desired result . . . so much so that maybe it was the researchers who were primed to get the result they expected instead of the participants who were primed to deliver it. On the other hand, a well-constructed list of mock trial voir dire questions is balanced to target bias against both sides of the case, not just one—any good consultant knows to make sure research questionnaires are written in a balanced manner. Similarly, at trial, both sides get to ask voir dire questions targeted to find bias against respective parties.

There is an exception, however. Voir dire questions that suggest information that may or may not come into the trial *can* be harmful. These questions can, in fact, prime participants to consider subject matter that they may not hear as evidence. I recall a personal injury lawsuit involving a fall. The plaintiff had a prior history of alcoholism, and at the time of jury selection, the judge had not yet decided if that information was going to be admissible. I was working with the plaintiff. My advice to the team: don't ask about it. The question itself could become evidence to the jurors, making this history a part of the trial even if the judge decided to exclude it, which he eventually did.

There is a difference between putting new apples in the basket of jurors' minds and simply looking to see what apples are already there. Preconceptions influence perceptions. And deeply held preconceptions are not created by a list of words or a question. They are created from life experiences. What people have learned in twenty, thirty, or forty years of life will have much more impact on their perception of a case story than anything you do, say, or ask. You do yourself no service by failing to understand what preconceptions are out there and how they may influence perceptions of your case story, especially in jury research exercises. It is in those exercises that you can later analyze preconceptions to see if there are any associations with verdict orientation—letting you know what information is the most important to gather in voir dire.

You do yourself no service by failing to understand what preconceptions are out there and how they may influence perceptions of your case story, especially in jury research exercises.

Voir dire questions do not plant opinions or experiences into jurors' minds, but they can bring to consciousness memories, ideas, or perceptions that a juror would not otherwise consider. What do I say to that? So what? The trial itself will do that anyway. Voir dire is a part of the strategic process. You want to get jurors thinking about your case in a manner that will elicit responses that will either join thoughts that would be positive to our position or reveal those that would be negative to it. That is the whole point. Is it not?

So go ahead and ask the question both in voir dire and in your jury research. The answer may just be the difference between knowing who to strike and who to allow in your group of decision makers.

Questions to Ask Yourself

- Are there questions I hesitate to ask in voir dire or jury research?

- Will those questions introduce new information or evidence into the trial or jury research that will otherwise not come into play?

- What do I risk by failing to get the information my questions will elicit?

3.5   Don't Believe Everything You Read on the Internet

I had the honor of being part of a discussion panel at the University of Pennsylvania's Inn of Court back in 2010. The question of the evening was whether or not it is practical, proper, and feasible to perform Internet searches on jurors to collect information for jury selection.

One of the other panelists was a law professor who took the names of a couple of the law students at the seminar and compiled an extensive dossier of information on each of them—all in just a few hours. We learned, among other things, where the students were raised, who their parents were, what organizations they belonged to, and what the property values of their parents' homes were.

So this begs the question, how useful can information gleaned from Internet searching be in jury selection? What kind of information can you discover about potential panel members that will help you decide the names to write on the strike list? Do you really want to open this potential Pandora's box of additional information?

In general, I can see both sides of the coin, and I have conducted jury selection both with and without such searches. From a logistical standpoint, it is often just not feasible. In many trial venues, the list of names is provided about five minutes before the jurors walk into the courtroom, and I feel lucky when I have juror questionnaires to review in advance, let alone the opportunity to perform an extensive Internet search.

Second, the process of selection is fast paced. You must make decisions in an instant. Even if you are given the list of jurors ahead of time and are physically able to spend the time searching the Internet for each person in your venire, you then face the task of wading through a tome of information at decision time. Too much information is not always a great asset and can potentially get the team nothing but inundated and confused.

Logistical issues aside, anyone can post anything on the Internet regardless of its truth. It is very possible that your search could direct you to misleading or even incorrect information. For example, in one of the searches performed on those unfortunate law students, the professor pulled up information that someone with the student's name was currently incarcerated in the State of Colorado. Needless to say, what he found was about a different person. We knew the student was not in that Colorado State Penitentiary, but sitting with us in West Philadelphia. In that case, the mistaken identity was a humorous side note. But in the real world, when you have no more information about a potential juror than their name and location, it won't be as easy to know whether information you find is actually about that person.

Moreover, it is impossible to know if the information is accurate even if you have found the right person. The issue brings us to research performed by Jeanne Logsdon and Karen Patterson,[17] who discovered that people are more likely to deceive when communicating business matters online than though other modes of communication. These findings certainly extend beyond the business context.

People don't put ugly pictures of themselves on Facebook—usually. Information a person posts about herself is more likely of an image she wants to project rather than one that may better reflect reality. Information posted by other people about your potential juror? The possibilities abound.

Regardless of the information that can be found online, you should focus your perceptions of jurors on how they interact with the courtroom environment, how they answer questions, and how they present themselves in the context in which they will be making their decisions. The courtroom is a face-to-face context, especially in regard to deliberations. Someone who is eloquent and opinionated while writing by himself in the comfort of his home may not have the same social capabilities when sitting in a room with eleven other people. For that reason, your primary focus should be on the person in the relevant context—the courtroom.

So, are Internet searches on jurors completely useless? Absolutely not. They can be very helpful if you leverage them properly with a healthy critical eye.

So if you have the opportunity, it is very helpful to search the names in your pool. From a big picture perspective, you can learn a lot in thirty or so minutes if a name and location pulls up blogs, LinkedIn, and Facebook profiles, etc. If a person posts pictures on Facebook or other social media, look at them. If they write posts that can be seen publicly, read them. Get a sense of what they care about in their lives by what they talk about online. In the searches I perform, I tend to discover strong political and religious affiliations, interests, family values, perspectives of current events, and the like. Of course, this is when the jurors make their social media postings publicly available (which a surprising number do). Keep in mind, however, the ethical guidelines that warn against searching beyond publicly available information as well as any associated rules enforced by the court.

So, are Internet searches on jurors completely useless? Absolutely not. They can be very helpful if you leverage them properly with a healthy critical eye.

If you find that a juror has a blog, by all means, have a read. It is certainly relevant to know what a person finds important enough to publish in the most public forum available, what they value enough to post on their social media feeds, what they reveal their interests to be by linking to specific-interest forums, or how they describe their occupation when networking.

---

17. Jeanne M. Logsdon & Karen D. W. Patterson, *Deception in Business Networks: Is It Easier to Lie Online?*, 90 JOURNAL OF BUSINESS ETHICS 537 (2009).

When I have a list of jurors ahead of time, I perform the search. Why not? Has the information been interesting? Almost always. Impactful? Sure. Has it ever guided a strike decision in isolation? Rarely. Of course, the most effective use of the information is to apply what you found on the Internet to how the juror presents in the courtroom.

Of course, the most effective use of the information is to apply what you found on the Internet to how the juror presents in the courtroom.

Therefore, you should view Internet searches in the context of "everything in moderation." If the opportunity presents itself, certainly avail yourself of it, but view it with full understanding of its limitations and beware of overreliance. The way people will interact in the jury room is still best determined by how they present themselves in the courtroom.

Questions to Ask Yourself

- What information am I able to get online about my jurors?

- What level of confidence do I have that my juror and the person I found online are the same person?

- To what extent am I relying on the information I found online?

- Am I getting the information in a format I can use without being overwhelmed?

- How does the information I received online about a juror comport with what I am seeing in the courtroom?

3.6   Know the Court

Most people believe that as a jury consultant, my only role in jury selection is to understand the inner workings of each juror and predict what decision he or she will make at the end of trial. While it is true that my job is to collect information about attitudes and backgrounds and determine the probability of a verdict orientation, my first jury selection task is much simpler: help keep the process organized and focused for the attorneys with whom I work.

The key to jury selection is to be prepared, not just with your profile, but with the knowledge of how the process will work, how it meshes with your overall trial strategy, and how you can smoothly navigate it.

Although it could potentially be the most important part of trial (you are, after all, putting together the group of people who will decide whether your client wins or loses), I have seen many attorneys put the *logistics* of jury selection on the back-burner in favor of other trial preparation. The key to jury selection is to be prepared, not just with your profile, but with the knowledge of how the process will work, how it meshes with your overall trial strategy, and how you can smoothly navigate it.

For most, the jury selection process entails a whirlwind of information even before the jurors walk into the room. Specifically, very few courts or judges within courts conduct jury selection in the same fashion:

- Are there juror questionnaires?
- How is voir dire conducted (the entire venire at once, one at a time, in groups)?
- Who conducts voir dire? The attorneys? The court? Some combination?
- If you conduct voir dire, what are the rules or boundaries (time, content, etc.)?
- How many strikes do you get?
- How many jurors will you have?
- Will there be alternates?
- Will the alternates know that they are alternates?
- Will alternates deliberate?

These are just a sampling of the questions you need organized in your head before jury selection begins, and you probably still have motions to argue.

The solution? Ask.

Yes, that is my earth-shattering advice. Simply ask the questions I listed above. Before the day of trial and, even better, before you begin to prepare your voir dire. While some answers may apply to all courtrooms within a jurisdiction (i.e., the number of jurors, alternates, and strikes), it is dangerous to assume a particular judge will handle jury selection the same way as another just because they reside in the same courthouse. Instead, call the clerk and discuss it. You just may learn some important details about the judge's preferences that will give you an edge in her courtroom.

Too many times, these simple phone calls don't get made and trial teams learn the jury selection processes while the selection is in motion. I see it all the time in court. It is obvious when it happens. Without having the full skinny ahead of time, trial teams needlessly make it harder on themselves, clouding their heads with logistics while they should be paying full attention to the potential jurors. Ideally, the only information the teams should learn on the fly in jury selection is information about the jurors themselves.

Being organized in jury selection is critical not only because it allows you to focus on making the right strike choices, but also because it is the first chance jurors have to see and develop impressions of you. Remember: you never get a second chance to make a first impression. Don't be fooled into believing that the trial begins with the openings. Jurors will begin to make judgments about you and your client the moment you step into the courtroom, the courthouse parking lot, the cafeteria, or bathroom. The jurors will notice when a trial team seems flustered and disorganized in jury selection—and not in a good way.

Questions to Ask Yourself

- Do I know the court's preferred procedure before I go to jury selection?

- Have I called the court to verify my understanding of the process?

- Am I prepared specifically to handle this court's process?

- Am I making a good first impression in front of the jurors by being organized in jury selection?

3.7 Use Juror Questionnaires When You Can

I am a big fan of juror questionnaires. In addition to what I can observe about a person in the courtroom, I find that there is much to be gleaned from what that person writes on a form and how they write it. Especially in complex or high-profile cases, juror questionnaires are extraordinarily helpful. They take a lot of burden and time off the voir dire process by having jurors provide information in a written format. You can uncover dangerous opinions without contaminating the panel and use voir dire as follow-up instead of as preliminary information gathering. I have seen efficient courts work with both counsel to use questionnaire information as a basis to strike jurors for cause (or other threshold issues, such as previous service, language difficulties, other disabilities, criminal convictions, etc.) before they come to the courtroom, avoiding the waste of time involved in questioning an ineligible juror.

I have found that jurors are more forthcoming with questionnaires. Without the social pressure of the judge, trial teams, and other jurors listening, jurors have more freedom to write what they *really* think and reveal those things that they would not otherwise say in an open proceeding, where social pressure may keep them quiet.

So juror questionnaires are great . . . *if* you are permitted to use them. A client once told me a story of a jury consultant who, like me, was a big advocate of juror questionnaires. My client had the consultant spend hours (translation: a lot of money) creating an extensive questionnaire for one of his cases. When the team submitted the questionnaire to the court, the judge revealed that he did not permit questionnaires in his court, and that my client's case would be no exception.

Again, ask!

Have this discussion directly with the judge so you can discuss the benefits of such a tool (e.g., for a court that allows attorney voir dire, it will save a lot of time). You may not get your wish, but, as ice hockey great Wayne Gretsky said, "You miss 100 percent of the shots you don't take."

I have also found that judges have been more willing to accept custom juror questionnaires when both sides agree to it. Therefore, this may be an area in which collaboration with an opponent could be beneficial for everyone.

If the court allows a custom questionnaire, you have to make sure you can use it to your benefit.

If the court allows a custom questionnaire, you have to make sure you can use it to your benefit. That means, in many cases, it has to be strategic, short, and sweet. If you are going to receive the completed questionnaires an hour before the voir dire process starts, long, detailed questionnaires will get you nothing but overwhelmed.

In some courts (Los Angeles and Las Vegas are examples), you may get the completed documents several days in advance. Obviously, with more time to peruse, you will have more freedom to add more detailed questions.

In some jurisdictions, courts have their own standard juror questionnaires that provide basic information. Some solely supply the basics: name, address, age, and occupation. Others provide more. I have selected juries in several jurisdictions that use different standard questionnaires for civil and criminal matters. In several Pennsylvania state courts, for instance, a two-sided form presents questions deemed for criminal matters on one side (e.g., have they been a victim of a crime, are they more/less likely to believe the testimony of a police officer than other witnesses, etc.). On the other side of the form, they are asked questions determined relevant to civil cases (e.g., do they have experience with the medical field, will they be unable to put sympathy aside, etc.). Jurors for all cases fill out both sides of the form.

In my experience with civil jury selections in venues that use these more comprehensive standard questionnaires, I noticed something that surprised me. Most attorneys ignore the questions that relate to the criminal trials and focus solely on the questions designed for civil matters.

They are missing some very good information.

There is much to learn about a person on these questionnaires beyond just the answers to questions targeted at your case. The fact is that questions related to criminal issues can yield some useful information even in a civil trial. For example, I have seen several questionnaires that ask if the potential juror has been the victim of a crime. If you are permitted, you may want to follow up with a juror who answers "yes." If the person had his wallet stolen once, that will not tell you much, but victims of serious or violent crimes may identify with a plaintiff's claim of victimization. This is especially true if the juror did not feel protected by the police or otherwise communicates a sense of helplessness. Both of these perceptions relate to a sense that authority establishments fail in their responsibility to people.

Similarly, I have seen questionnaires that ask if the person has been arrested or is close to someone who has been arrested. Again, negative experiences with authority typically translate into a bias against any and all parties that represent authority in the courtroom. Corporate defendants beware. On the other hand, in civil cases in which the defendant is an individual, such as in a car accident, an affirmative answer to this question may translate into identifying with being wrongly accused.

There is much to learn about a person on these questionnaires beyond just the answers to questions targeted at your case.

In addition to the content of the answers, it is important to look at the form in general. Was it filled out correctly or fully?

How well someone follows the instructions on the form can tell you something about that person. First, you must acknowledge that the potential juror may not have the level of literacy needed to understand and complete the questionnaire. In 2009, the United States Department of Education released federal statistics that more than 32 million adults in the United States (about 14 percent) have very low literacy skills. This is not just an issue about completing a juror questionnaire—it should also raise flags about the potential juror's ability to navigate trial evidence that involves contracts, charts, or other documents the juror would need to read, comprehend, and evaluate. Many people in such a position would not come out and reveal literacy problems in open court. That is most likely embarrassing, and most of us rightfully are wary about asking such a question to a panel and being seen as insulting or derogatory.

If the quality of a questionnaire elicits concern about a juror's literacy, or any other sensitive topic for that matter, open the door to discuss the matter in private with the judge and counsel. Do not—I repeat—*do not* call an individual out in the public forum. That will quickly leave that juror (and others) with an unfavorable impression of you. Either ask at sidebar if there is anything that would make it difficult to serve as a juror in a case involving written contracts, for example, or come right out and say that you had some difficulty following his or her questionnaire answers and ask if there is anything that was a concern about filling it out. If you ask sensitively and privately, you are more likely to get an honest answer.

Second, an incorrectly filled-out questionnaire may give you an indication of a person's attention to detail. In trials, the devil is often in the details, and knowing whether a person pays attention to the "fine print" can be important.

Finally, a lax attitude toward a court-provided document may tell you something about a person and her willingness to follow other kinds of instructions. If a person can't follow the simple instructions on the questionnaire, that may reflect on her willingness as a juror to follow other, more complex instructions, like those the judge will provide related to the law.

I remember one trial in Philadelphia in which an overwhelming majority of people did not follow the instructions to complete the survey. That's right, an *overwhelming* majority. We were a corporate defendant in a construction accident case, and the instructions on the law would be very important in our very technical defense. These were clearly not jurors who followed instructions. The questionnaires were the straw that broke the camel's back. With my encouragement, the client settled the case before we started voir dire.

So whether the court has a standard questionnaire or you are able to submit your own to the court, what do you do with that stack of completed papers? A clear sense of what you are looking for is critical so you can quickly review each document and identify those with responses riskiest to your case. My advice: get help.

It is impossible to simultaneously pay attention to the proceedings, participate in motion arguments, and read all of the critical information in those questionnaires. Regardless of who it is (a trusted consultant, associate, or partner), make sure you assign a person to read all of the relevant information in the questionnaire. Whoever is reviewing the questionnaires should filter to you only the information that would have an impact on your decision-making. That way, you fully leverage the benefit of the information gleaned from the questionnaire and focus on what you need to focus on—moving ahead quickly and efficiently.

As much as a simple juror questionnaire may appear to contain little information, don't be deceived. If you take full advantage, it can provide a high-level picture of important juror characteristics and can offer you a more fruitful foundation to explore in voir dire.

Questions to Ask Yourself

- Does the court have a standard questionnaire?
- What information can I get from the court's standard questionnaire, both in terms of content and the manner in which jurors fill it out?
- Will a custom questionnaire benefit my case?
- Will opposing counsel agree to a mutually developed custom questionnaire?
- Will the judge agree to a custom questionnaire?
- Will I be able to have jurors fill out the juror questionnaires ahead of time?
- Does the length and format of my questionnaire make it easy to use considering the court's jury selection process?
- Do I have the help I need to use the questionnaires effectively?

3.8   Construct Voir Dire in Context

Keeping voir dire organized first and foremost involves knowing what the voir dire process looks like in a given courtroom.

The judge may conduct voir dire based on the courts own predetermined questions, questions submitted by counsel, or a combination of the two, and not permit you to say much of anything. All you can do is listen and keep track of the little bit of information you get. Obviously, knowing this ahead of time prevents you from wasting time and money creating questions you'll never get to ask.

If you are permitted to ask questions, the first critical issue is not what questions you will ask, but *how* you will be permitted to ask them.

There are several ways voir dire may be conducted. You may ask questions to a large group, a small group, individually, or anywhere in between. Regardless, the fact is that you need to know how voir dire is conducted so you can construct your questions in a way that maximizes the process.

In a federal antitrust case, I was helping a team that had already created their voir dire. They provided me their list the morning of the jury selection. The problem I noticed was that the questions, while good in terms of content, were open-ended. The voir dire was to be conducted with the whole venire at once. While open-ended questions are recommended for individual voir dire, you can't ask sixty people at once an open-ended question. You need to ask questions in a "Yes" or "No" format and then potentially follow up.

While I quickly retooled the list, the attorney already had the questions in his mind as written and needed to pause and relearn each question. He clearly was uncomfortable during voir dire. It looked like it was the first time he had seen the questions—because it was.

If you are permitted to ask questions, the first critical issue is not what questions you will ask, but how you will be permitted to ask them.

Another critical mistake I see in voir dire is the length of time attorneys spend asking questions, especially when given an unlimited amount of time.

I have experienced several trials where there were no time limits for voir dire, and opposing counsel took advantage to a fault. In one insurance dispute trial in Los Angeles, we interviewed twelve jurors at a time. I was assisting the defense. Plaintiff's counsel spent the better part of a day interviewing just those first twelve people. When it was my client's turn, he had three critical pieces of information we wanted him to obtain from each person. He got up, engaged the panel, and was sitting down again within thirty minutes. He spent just enough time developing a rapport and getting the information we needed. This process was repeated several times until we had enough eligible people to empanel the jury. By the end, we had the key information we needed to make our strikes. We presented ourselves as cordial, professional, and organized.

However, when plaintiff's counsel rose from his chair to conduct additional voir dire of new panel members who replaced those stricken for cause—and even when he rose to give his opening—I could see the jurors visibly slump down in their seats and roll their eyes. While admittedly I can't know what they were thinking, their expressions seemed to say: "Oh, boy. How long are we going to be listening to this guy *this* time?"

I remember other trials in Las Vegas and Fort Worth in which attorneys asked questions of their respective panels for two days. I heard jurors make substantially unflattering comments about counsel and the process in both instances. In the Las Vegas trial, one potential juror yelled out in discontent to the judge, "Do you ever stop them?" He was not selected.

Less is often more.

Less is often more. Developing rapport and collecting the most relevant information does not mean you have to engage each person in a long dialogue. First, you will collect too much information for you to actually use. Second, while jurors expect you to be a professional and friendly, they do not expect you to be their friend. I prefer attorneys asking one or two rapport-building questions. Otherwise, my philosophy of voir dire is like my philosophy of grocery shopping: take the time you need to get what you need, and then get out of there.

My personal favorite rapport-building question is "What do you like to do in your spare time?" It is a friendly topic about which most people have a response, and when they don't, that is telling about that person as well. I find hobbies provide good information about a person and his or her values. Once the rapport-building question is out there, it is time to move on to the key strategic questions that will give you the information you need to make strikes.

With a carefully constructed voir dire, you can get the job done quickly and efficiently. Jurors will consider you organized and on top of your game and will thank you for respecting their time.

Questions to Ask Yourself

- What is the voir dire procedure in this courtroom?

- Do I get to ask any questions?

- Should my questions be open-ended or of the "yes" or "no" variety?

- What information do I need to get from the jurors to make my striking decisions?

- Do the questions I am asking in voir dire get me the information I need?

- Do the questions I am asking help me develop rapport without going overboard?

- Am I respecting jurors' time?

3.9 Keep Track of Your Jurors

After you have collected all of the juror information you are going to get via Internet searches, questionnaires, voir dire, and any other mode of data collection, the question becomes: now what do you do with all of the information?

Of course, there is no "one-size-fits-all" solution to tracking juror information during voir dire. Different people are comfortable with different strategies. Some people write notes on regular lined paper, some create charts of where jurors are sitting, some use computerized systems. I personally like using a "high-tech" charting system that employs sticky notes and a highlighter pen. I like sticky notes because they can be moved and removed throughout the process as people are stricken from the venire. They keep my charts clutter free and clear of anything I won't use. The highlighter calls attention to the information I consider most relevant to the striking decisions about each person.

Using my sticky pad and highlighter method, I employ a two-step grading system. As the first step, I use the traditional A through F grading system. A's are, from a profiling perspective, ideal jurors (who we will probably lose to the other side's strikes), and F's are those unlikely to find for us no matter what we argue.

The second step evaluates the impact a particular juror will likely have on the rest of the panel (L for low; M for moderate; H for high). If a person is articulate, knowledgeable about the subject matter, or otherwise demonstrates a presence among the juror pool, I mark that person as likely having a high impact. With the two-step grading system, I can focus on the D's, F's, and H's and then make a decision.

An organized system provides you a clear picture of where you should focus at decision time.

Whatever your chosen system is, there are a few simple principles that apply across the board to keep the task of tracking juror information as simple as possible:

1. *Weed out the irrelevant.* If you try to capture everything each juror says, you are not only more likely to miss something important, you are simply not going to be able to get through the tome of information quickly when you have to make decisions. Know ahead of time what you are looking for and listen carefully for it. Let everything else go.

2. *Focus primarily on the information that indicates your adverse jurors.* I have to remind even the most seasoned trial attorneys that jury selection is a misnomer. It would be more accurate to call it jury deselection. You can't keep. You can only boot. If you are focused on the information that is good about jurors, you are taking precious attention away from the task at hand—to identify your worst.

3. *Get help.* I said it before, and I will say it again. Unless you are not permitted to do anything in jury selection except be a spectator while the judge conducts voir dire, it is too much for one person to both develop rapport with the jury and keep track of the information provided. Whether a partner, associate, paralegal, or a consultant, assign someone you trust the task of documenting the relevant information to discuss with you later.

An organized system provides you a clear picture of where you should focus at decision time. While one last review of everyone in the final set of jurors is important, a good system lets you know where to focus by highlighting the information determined to be most relevant in a manner that is accessible. In the small window of time you are allowed to make striking decisions, having a clean process will ensure your final decisions are based on critical consideration of the most pertinent juror information.

Questions to Ask Yourself

- Do I have an organized system for keeping track of jurors that works for me?

- Should I be focused on keeping track of the jurors in jury selection or should I be attending to the people on the panel?

- If I need to keep my attention on the people in the panel, do I have a trusted person to keep track of the relevant juror information for me?

- What information is truly relevant for me to make a strike decision?

- Am I too focused on jurors who are good for me?

PART FOUR

MANAGING WITNESSES

4.1 Make a Case that Fits Your Client

You can't change the core of who a human being is. No witness coach, theatrical trainer, or lawyer will be able to accomplish this, no matter what kind of witness preparation they perform.

Research shows that core personality traits remain stable over time. A study by David Buss in 1994 looked at the stability of personality specifically within the context of solving adaptive problems and handling situations of conflict.[1] Buss conducted a longitudinal study of 100 newly married couples and followed them for four years. What better context to study how people resolve conflict over time than marriage? Buss concluded that personality remains stable because people, over time, develop psychological mechanisms or patterns of interactions to adapt to life situations or solve problems. These mechanisms provide them with "success" in navigating those situations and solving those problems. People will consistently resort to these adaptive strategies time and time again, generalizing them to each new context or challenge, creating a consistent pattern of interacting with situations and with people—otherwise known as "personality."

As in marriage, witnesses too will resort to what has made them successful in the past and apply that to the manner in which they navigate their testimony. With that in mind, the goal of witness preparation is not to change people or engage in a futile attempt to modify their core personalities. Instead, the goals of witness preparation are to first identify the witness's natural communication style, and then determine how her pattern of problem-solving interacts with the unnatural context of giving testimony.

I have received many calls from attorneys asking for help in making their central witness reflect the image they need to fit their case themes. When I then meet with the witness, I sometimes find that the theme of the case is totally incompatible

---

1. David M. Buss, *Personality Evoked: The Evolutionary Psychology of Stability and Change, in* CAN PERSONALITY CHANGE? (T. F. Heatherton & J. L. Weinberger eds. 1994).

with who that person, at her core, truly is. In these cases, it is not only the witness who needs work; it is the bigger picture case strategy as well.

When dealing with a case in which one witness's testimony is critical, it is extremely important to have a good understanding of who that person is and make sure the strategy you choose takes that person into account.

I remember a case in Milwaukee in which I was called in to prepare a doctor for trial. He was a primary care physician accused of failing to diagnose liver cancer. I watched his video deposition. The doctor was quirky, to say the least. He came across as socially awkward and robotic. He was definitely the kind of doctor who was into the science of medicine. He had that intellectual, nerdy quality about him. When I met with him, I began by having a conversation about the case and how he was reacting to it. Through this conversation, I developed a sense of how he communicated regularly, outside of the testimony context. Still quirky, but not so robotic. I got a sense of where the work was needed and gained an understanding of what was not changeable, but just *him*.

When dealing with a case in which one witness's testimony is critical, it is extremely important to have a good understanding of who that person is and make sure the strategy you choose takes that person into account.

In this case, there were two areas that needed concentrated effort. The first was with the doctor, helping him get comfortable in his own skin while in the foreign communication context of testimony. Once he was able to put his perspective into bigger picture messages and gain familiarity with the cadence of testimony, the robotic characteristic of his answers abated, and we were left with a quirky, yet endearing, science guy.

The second area of feedback was working with the trial team to provide case messages that embraced our doctor. Our message became one of "science-based medicine," which fit well with the image of this quirky science guy we had as a client. In other words, we tailored our arguments to match his thought process: in the empirical research associated with the symptoms the patient presented and resulting diagnostic impressions. Verdict: No negligence.

Before witness preparation can be effective, you must first understand what can be affected.

In essence, before witness preparation can be effective, you must first understand what can be affected. It is in the space between the core of the human being and the reaction to giving testimony where witness preparation work can be the most fruitful. Dealing with just the surface (i.e., how she sits, where she looks) helps, but does not get to the real issue. Trying to change core elements of a person's disposition is an exercise in futility. In fact, it works in litigation about as well as it does in marriage.

The point is this: it is not about changing a person to fit your case. It is about making a case that fits the person you put on the stand.

Questions to Ask Yourself

- How would I describe my key witness's core personality?

- Does my case strategy conflict with my key witness's core personality?

- How can I construct a case message that comports with my key witness's core personality?

- How does my witness react to the stress of testimony?

- Am I using witness preparation to manage the anxiety that affects my witness's communication, or am I engaging in a fruitless attempt to change her core personality?

4.2 Set the Right Foundation for Your Witness

While every witness preparation session I conduct differs depending on the needs, communicative issues, and messages of a particular witness, there is one step I take with just about every witness with whom I work. I specifically ask the following question: "If I were a juror in your case, what are the three main concepts or ideas I need to learn *from you and your testimony?*" The answers are often astonishing.

I have seen defendant doctors in malpractice actions who answer this question in a manner that has nothing to do with the medical treatment they provided, plaintiffs who deliver opinions that they learned from the case experts about a product's defect, and corporate executives who just stare at me blankly with no idea what to say. When I turn to the attorneys to ask what they think are the witness's main messages, the answers are usually better, but it is often clear that counsel has not thought about these messages from this ten-thousand-foot conceptual vantage point either.

While it is the witnesses' primary job to listen to a question and answer that question with literal truth, to do that effectively, they must clearly understand the foundation of their core messages. This is not to say that attorneys feed witnesses their messages void of the witnesses' input. Instead, as you talk through the story in witnesses' own words, whittle the information down to its overarching points. This helps witnesses get their own thoughts organized in an important way.

While it is the witnesses' primary job to listen to a question and answer that question with literal truth, to do that effectively, they must clearly understand the foundation of their core messages.

When witnesses testify while understanding what is truly important, they feel more prepared. When they feel more prepared, they feel more confident. When they feel more confident, they are focused on the question and not on their discomfort. When they are focused on the question, they give better, cleaner, and more accurate testimony.

Importantly, when you discuss the witness's core message, you also discuss the limitations of those messages. In other words, the witness needs to know what he should leave to the testimony of others. The best examples of this typically concern knowledgeable fact witnesses who don't know where their fact testimony ends and the expert testimony begins. This is an issue I see often with doctor defendants in medical malpractice cases. Take the orthopedic surgeon in Las Vegas accused of malpractice after his patient suffered complications following the reduction of a fracture. After suffering the complication, the patient went to a different provider, who performed multiple and painful revision surgeries. The patient, with full support of the subsequent provider, accused the defendant of botching the original surgery and causing this inevitable painful course of revisions.

While the defendant surgeon conceded that his patient suffered a known complication after surgery, he believed strongly that the medical records showed that it was the process of revision performed by the subsequent surgeon that was actually botched, preventing the patient's proper recovery. The defendant surgeon was able to explain clearly and with authority what exactly the subsequent provider had done wrong in the revision process and why those errors were the true cause of the plaintiff's condition. He, not surprisingly, surmised that this was the reason that subsequent surgeon was so very helpful in the plaintiff's litigation.

Of course, this orthopedic surgeon was an expert in his field, not only about the surgery he performed, but about complications and the treatment and revisions of those complications. In the case of his defense, though, his role was to speak solely to what he saw, what he heard, what he thought, and what he did in that operating room on that day of the initial surgery, based on the foundation of his experience and education.

Regardless of his impressive knowledge and the effectiveness with which he could explain the medicine behind his assertion that the other provider was to blame for much of the plaintiff's lasting deficits, that was not his role. That was the role of an expert. That is what experts do.

This was an extremely difficult concept for this defendant to grasp, and so we worked with him until he grasped it. He was not accustomed to stepping aside and letting others speak to his own area of expertise. It was clear that if we had not directly defined the limits of his testimony, he would have launched fully into his theory at trial, causing him to appear overly defensive, deflecting blame on other providers instead of focusing on confidence in his own care. Bullet dodged.

Without a basic foundation of how their messages fit into the entire case, witnesses flounder and flail in the rough seas of cross-examination.

Do your witnesses a favor. Throw them a life preserver before they have to testify in the form of discussing their core messages and the limits of those messages. Without a basic foundation of how their messages fit into the entire case, witnesses flounder and flail in the rough seas of cross-examination.

Of course, keeping messages clear for witnesses is the first step to keeping them clear for jurors. When the witness feels organized and prepared by clearly understanding the size and shape of their particular message and can get rid of the anxiety-induced clutter in her mind, she is more likely to communicate in an organized fashion, making it easier for jurors to understand. People mentally organize the information they take in. They categorize concepts. They put the pieces of a story together in a way that makes sense for them. Having a witness who communicates organized concepts will go far in making sure the jurors organize the messages in a similar manner.

When preparing for depositions or trial, have a sense of the three specific messages you believe need to come from each witness. During preparation, ask the witness her perception of her key messages and see if it comports with your perspective. If it does, great. If it doesn't, discussion needs to ensue to make sure both you and your witness are on the same page and that the messages you are considering for your case really comport with the evidence that will come in through testimony. Again, this is not telling the witness what to say. It is making sure you are presenting the case in a manner that is true to the witness's messages and then helping her relay those messages clearly.

Questions to Ask Yourself

- What do I think my witness's three high-level messages are?

- What does my witness understand to be her three high-level messages?

- Are my idea of my witness's messages and my witness's idea of her messages in line?

- Where are the boundaries of my witness's messages?

- Does my witness understand where the boundaries of her messages lie?

4.3   Ask the Right Questions Off the Stand

A lasting lesson I learned about witness preparation happened when I was just starting out as a jury consultant. I was working on a pharmaceutical patent case in which expert witness testimony was critical. The trial team brought me in because they were concerned about how their key expert would come across to the jury. They said that his content was good, but his nonverbal communication was a real problem. They were afraid that the expert could inadvertently send the message that he had no confidence in his own opinion.

This expert was, quite possibly, the smartest person I had ever met. He had multiple PhDs and was the preeminent expert in his field. He knew the chemistry at issue in the case possibly better than anyone in the world. We went through some practice direct and cross-examinations with him. His answers were perfect, but his demeanor was miserable. He was fidgety. His voice kept dropping to a whisper. He was just so blatantly anxious.

I went through the basic witness-training techniques, explaining to him that jurors are simply people who want to understand, just like the students he taught at his university. Didn't help. We went through each critical topic area and identified the basic key messages he could rely on throughout testimony. Didn't help. I gave him the basic advice:

1. You don't have to accept the examiner's language—rephrase in your own words if you are uncomfortable with "yes" or "no."

2. Remember that your audience is not the questioner, but the folks in the jury box.

3. If the questioner is nasty, take a breath to separate the content of the question from the tone and insinuation, and then answer it.

4. Your only job is to listen to the question and answer it.

5. Etc.

Didn't help. Didn't help. Didn't help. Didn't help.

The "ah-ha" moment came when we were on a break and the science expert and jury expert were able to take a breath. Chatting about the day's events, I said to him, "Dr. A., I am at a total loss. You seem to know the answer to every question with absolutely no problem, but there just seems to be something bothering you, and I can't figure out what it is. What could be the worst thing they could possibly ask you at this trial?" Dr. A. immediately said, "I am not worried about any of the questions at all. I know this material and this case well enough to know I can handle whatever question they throw at me."

I tried again. "If you know the material, and there is nothing they can ask that you can't handle, what is causing you to appear so worried? You are not acting worried while we are talking right now, so I know that is not how you normally communicate."

Dr. A. looked down as if he was ashamed. After a moment, he spoke. "Well, there are two things," he said. "First, I am dyslexic, and I am worried that they will give me something to read and I will look stupid if I mess up the words. Second, I have a problem with my prostate, and I am worried about having to go to the bathroom. Jurors will think I am taking all those breaks to get the answers to questions." Bingo. It was such a basic question, and I had finally asked it the right way.

I then asked, "Did you tell the attorneys this?" He hadn't. It never came up, and it was too embarrassing for him to mention unsolicited. So we discussed it with the trial team and decided that if we bring the issues up to the jury in the beginning, they will understand why he needed to take breaks, forgive any misreads of documents, and be all the more impressed that this expert made the academic and professional achievements he had with a learning disability. Having these worries out in the open and putting a comfortable solution in place, the weight was lifted from Dr. A.'s shoulders. In the next session, he showed dramatic improvement.

Sometimes litigators get so mired down by the facts and arguments of the case, they forget to check in with the people of the case.

The moral of the story is this: sometimes litigators get so mired down by the facts and arguments of the case, they forget to check in with the *people* of the case. All witnesses—whether plaintiffs, defendants, experts, or whomever—are human beings put in a very uncomfortable and unnatural situation. Don't forget to check in with them on a human level.

I tell this story to just about every witness I prepare, and then I ask, "Is there anything related to the case facts or otherwise that is bothering you or that you have been thinking about as you get ready to testify for this trial?" If you ask the right question, you may be surprised by what you learn.

Questions to Ask Yourself

- Have I checked in with the people who are testifying in my case on a human level?

- Have I asked my witness if there is anything causing her stress about testifying?

4.4   Teach Balance in Deposition

I have heard it said that there are only four good answers a witness can give in a deposition: "Yes," "No," "I don't know," and "I don't remember." I wholeheartedly disagree with this strategy.

Instructing a witness to essentially refuse to provide any real answers to adverse questions in deposition can backfire in multiple ways. Not the least of which is the fact that this advice essentially allows opposing counsel to testify for witnesses on the record. Think of it this way: when you read a deposition and the answers only confirm or deny the question, the content of that deposition comes from the question. The question becomes the evidence. The wording of the question comes from the other side.

There is another important issue to consider as well—witnesses typically don't like to be on that short of a leash. And they can get angry.

Instructing a witness to essentially refuse to provide any real answers to adverse questions in deposition can backfire in multiple ways.

Several years back, I did some witness work in a string of Alabama cases for a defendant insurance company accused of unfairly raising premiums once insured members were locked into their policies. Witnesses were deposed repeatedly over the series of cases. One witness, in particular, was very popular with the plaintiffs' counsel. He was an actuary who evaluated risk associated with each insured to determine premium rates. Opposing counsel often requested him by name. Let's call him Mr. A.

When I reviewed Mr. A.'s past videotaped depositions, it became clear why plaintiffs requested to depose him time and time again. He was terrible. He sat with arms crossed, snarling one word answers or snide comments. As a result, Mr. A. came off as having a complete disregard toward the human beings behind the risk analyses he performed. This was exactly the image of the insurance company the plaintiffs wanted on the record.

In a witness preparation session with Mr. A. and his trial team, we reviewed some of those videotapes. Then I did what had not been done before: I asked Mr. A. what *he* thought. Here is a paraphrased glimpse of our conversation.

Q: So, what do you think about the testimony you just watched?

A: I think it was terrible.

Q: What was terrible about it?

A: The way I keep answering questions with just one word.

Q: If you think it is terrible, why do you keep doing that?

A: Because that is what they (*motions toward trial team*) told me to do.

When I looked over at the team, I saw a room full of stunned faces.

As it turns out, Mr. A. actually had the tendency to be long-winded. He also was not well versed in the art of human communication (not unusual for the analytical type he was). That said, he knew his business and had good messages to share. Because of concerns about his gruff personality, however, the trial team told him, many depositions prior, to answer either "yes" or "no." So that was exactly what Mr. A. did. He sacrificed his key messages to follow counsel's literal instructions. And boy, was he angry about it.

Much of the time I spent in witness preparation with Mr. A. was spent repairing communications between him and the trial team. It became clear that much of Mr. A's anger in depositions, often interpreted as irritation toward plaintiff's counsel (or worse, contempt for the plaintiffs), was actually directed to the short leash he felt he was on, perceiving that he was not permitted to give complete and truthful answers to the questions.

So the conundrum is clear—how do you get a witness to answer a question and nothing but the question, but still make sure that the language on the record comes from the right side of the case and help the witness feel like she has the freedom to give her own answers? The answer is balance.

In another matter, I worked with some witnesses in a commercial case involving the privatization of a publicly traded company. The witnesses were very intelligent and high powered. But they were fish out of water when giving testimony. The group of them fell relatively evenly on the polar ends of the testimony spectrum. Specifically, some would flatly say "yes" to any question that had an element of truth in it, even if the context of the question was completely off-base. Others went off on tangents, engaging in debate and working hard to convince opposing counsel of their position. I had my work cut out for me.

While the testifying tendencies of these witnesses—as well our insurance actuary, Mr. A.—were disparate, the primary issue for preparation was the same. Specifically, there is a balance that every witness needs to understand how to strike. That balance is to find that sweet spot between one word answers and dissertations of gratuitous information.

The key to this balance is threefold: first, make sure the witness understands the difference between answering and explaining. Second, make sure the witness knows that rules are meant to be broken. Third, tell the witness to pick his battles. A witness who is grounded in these three skills is on the road to being well-prepared.

There is a balance that every witness needs to understand how to strike. That balance is to find that sweet spot between one word answers and dissertations of gratuitous information.

Point One: Understand the difference between answering versus explaining.

There is a difference between adding context and providing an explanation. The first is helpful during cross-examination or deposition, the second is not. Take the following exchange, for example, in the company privatization case:

Question

Would you agree with me that despite the fact that you were more profitable in 2008 than 2007, you represented to investors a poorer financial report in 2008?

Explanation

Well, in 2008, the United States was facing financial difficulties as a result of a crash in the real estate market. That crash affected the entire economy of the country, including the businesses that resided within it . . . (*continue for several pages*).

Answer

While we did bring in more profits in 2008 than 2007, that increased profitability was not able to overcome the economic crash of that year. Therefore, we did have a poorer financial report, which we communicated to the investors.

Both responses tell the correct story. But only one begins and ends with an answer to the question; the other meanders into an explanation that sounds like an evasive side story.

Point Two: Remember that rules are meant to be broken.

I have noticed that there are times when I give advice to witnesses and they, so eager for the help, take that advice to be absolute or applicable to every situation. I remember providing one particularly anxious witness the standard instruction to periodically look toward the jury in efforts to develop rapport. During practice cross, however, he didn't even glance toward the attorney asking him questions. Instead, he kept staring at me, his mock juror. I had to explain to him that addressing the jurors does not mean ignoring the questioner or staring the jury down. If it doesn't feel natural, it doesn't look natural. Truth be told, it was creepy.

No strategy or rule is absolute. They are tools to be pulled from the toolbox when they apply. Good preparation is helping witnesses use their own good judgment about when to use a strategy and when to let it go. Which brings us to our next point.

Point Three: Pick your battles.

It is awkward to restate every single question in a cross-examination or deposition. So when do you break the rule of making sure the language on the record is your own? When the correct answer really is "yes" or "no" or when the subject matter of the question is simply not important to the case. I have found that with the proper contextual application, most witnesses can understand the middle ground and apply it.

So when our actuary, Mr. A., was finally given the opportunity to have a *real dialogue* with the team, he gained a better understanding of the lawsuit and his place in it. He realized that he could, and should, add context to answers as long as it was directly responsive to the posed question. In the end, it worked out for both trial team and witness. In subsequent depositions, Mr. A. did much better and provided helpful messages for the defense. Plaintiffs eventually stopped asking for him, which is really what we all wanted in the first place.

Similarly, in the company privatization matter, work on balance in deposition brought the witnesses on both ends of the spectrum into that helpful sweet spot. They did a great job. Their testimony stood on its own. And they won their case.

Questions to Ask Yourself

- Is the manner in which I am instructing my witness to testify allowing my witness's own testimony to be on the record?

- Am I so nervous about this witness that I want him to say as little as possible on the record?

- Does my witness have the tendency to provide long-winded answers or try to win the case with every question?

- Does my witness understand the difference between an answer and an explanation?

- Am I providing my witness with multiple testifying tools so he can use good judgment on when to use them?

- Am I giving my witness testifying tools that help him feel and look natural in giving testimony?

4.5   Understand Culture and Communication Values

The courtroom has its own culture. It encompasses within it distinct language, ritual, and communicative values. It is a difficult cultural environment for any witness unfamiliar with its distinct language, ritual, and values. It takes work for witnesses to learn when they are supposed to speak, how they are supposed to answer, and what their role is. In many ways, the courtroom asks witnesses to suspend just about everything they have learned about normal human interaction and relearn communication in its culture: Speak only when asked a question. Remember that even though the question comes from the attorney, the answer is meant for the jury. Don't overlap language with that of the questioner. Don't say anything beyond what is specifically asked. Etc., etc.

So what happens when the cultural communication values within a particular context like the courtroom conflict with the cultural communication values that a person has developed over a lifetime? As I describe in my 2010 article, "The Cultural Theory of Plane Crashes and Witness Disasters," when not addressed, this conflict can lead to catastrophe.[2]

In many ways, the courtroom asks witnesses to suspend just about everything they have learned about normal human interaction and relearn communication in its culture.

There is a social theory about communicative values developed by Geert Hofstede, a theorist and researcher on organizational cultures.[3] A critical tenet of his theory is known as power distance, which explains cultural values as they relate to communication across hierarchical levels. Hofstede theorizes that cultures with a high power distance value are those in which people communicate in deference to authority, even in times of disagreement. The hierarchical division is of utmost importance, and language is a method of showing respect for it. On the other hand, cultures with a low power distance value show less deference to authority. People across any perceived level of hierarchy speak candidly and directly with one another and are more willing to voice their disagreements.

Hofstede's theory also addresses the value of individualism versus collectivism in the manner in which people communicate. In other words, does the culture value the individual or the group, and how does that manifest itself in verbalizations? Is it the "I" or the "we"?

---

2. Melissa M. Gomez, *The Cultural Theory of Plane Crashes and Witness Disasters,* THE LEGAL INTELLIGENCER (December 20, 2010).
3. Geert Hofstede, *National Cultures in Four Dimensions: A Research-Based Theory of Cultural Differences Among Nations,* 13 INTERNATIONAL STUDIES OF MANAGEMENT & ORGANIZATION 46 (1983).

The hard-to-believe aspect of this social theory is the extent to which it becomes so engrained in a person's value system. Strong attachment to that cultural communicative value can prevail, even to a person's detriment.

In his book *Outliers,* Malcolm Gladwell connects Hoftede's theory to instances of plane crashes that were caused simply by the communicative barriers between two opposing cultures.[4] That's right, plane crashes. Plural. As in, more than one. The crash of Avianca's Flight 52 is an example. On Thursday, January 25, 1990, the plane, which originated in Bogotá, Columbia, was approaching John F. Kennedy International Airport. The plane's pilot, from the Colombian high power distance culture did not demand air traffic control to permit his plane to land immediately nor did he directly communicate that the plane was running out of fuel. The air traffic controller, from the American low power distance culture, did not perceive the undertone of urgency—he was operating under his cultural expectation of direct communication and so assumed that the plane was low on fuel, but not in an emergency situation.

It was an emergency situation. The result was that the plane crashed into the small village of Cove Neck, New York, on the north shore of Long Island, killing seventy-three of the 158 passengers on board.

The same kind of communicative clash of cultures can happen in litigation. I remember a Korean witness whose cultural values conflicted with those of the courtroom. He was a doctor, sued in a medical malpractice case. The Korean culture is one that is in line with the high power distance value. In accordance, the defendant doctor was respectful and agreeable to his attorneys throughout preparation, keeping his head down in deference. After all, they were the authority in the litigation context. The problem was that at deposition, the defendant doctor perceived opposing counsel through the same cultural lens. Congruent with his high power distance value, he was agreeable with opposing counsel to the extent that he conceded all accusations made about him, regardless of the fact that they were not true. The end result was a deposition riddled with false testimony, caused solely by the witness's difficulty with adjusting his own value system in a manner that allowed him to disagree with the accusations made against him. I was called in for damage control between the deposition and trial, but by then the problem was already on the record.

Moreover, in some high power distance cultures, the concept of litigation in general is beyond comprehension. I have prepared more than one foreign doctor who simply could not believe that he had been sued. That simply doesn't happen in high power distance cultures because of the respect for the authority of the medical community and the lack of value of the individual over the community that benefits from a physician's medical service.

---

4. Malcolm Gladwell, Outliers: The Story of Success (2008).

National Institute for Trial Advocacy

While it is easy to view these issues as applying primarily to foreign witnesses, communicative values are relevant to all testifiers. Different people have different communication styles, reactions to anxiety, and views of authority. They have their ingrained strategies for adapting to situations and solving problems. Understanding these variables and how they can wreak havoc when applied to testimony may head off trouble down the road.

I recall a Boston contract dispute in which shareholders of a company claimed that they were cheated out of money when the company was sold. The key witness for the defense was a wealthy businessman who buys and sells companies. He runs businesses. He respected authority and hierarchy from the perspective of being at the top of it. This witness had a communicative value of taking charge with his language. He didn't answer questions. He asked them. This was the way he found success in business. This was the way he thought he would find success in litigation as well. He was wrong.

Like the Korean doctor, this witness's deposition was a disaster, but for reasons on the opposite end of the spectrum. He came across as believing he was above the rules, refusing to answer the question at hand and providing the information he wanted to instead. The worst part was that he thought he had hit a home run in his deposition. Convincing him otherwise took the feedback of the participants of a large mock trial for whom we played some of the video.

It is important not only to understand the communicative problems, but also to understand the values that lie beneath them.

For witnesses like this, the work of improving testimony and simply getting him to answer a question was not going to be fruitful by our simply telling him what to do. No one told this man what to do. Instead, the fruitful route was identifying the situation for what it was, defining his communication style, and talking through the reasons it 1) had brought him success as a business man and 2) would bring him defeat in litigation. This process was about understanding this witness's communicative values and reflecting them back to him so he could have a greater understanding of why his natural communication style was what it was. It worked for him in *his* world. But he needed to understand why it would not work in the world of litigation. The process was ultimately about redefining what a "win" is and what "power" in testimony is. It was about getting to the same result, just in a different manner in the testimony context.

In essence, it is important not only to understand the communicative problems, but also to understand the values that lie beneath them. Where has the communication style of a witness been of benefit? Is it ingrained culturally or has it been learned from past experience? Of course, where the witness was raised, either internationally or domestically, is relevant. Having direct conversations about communication within that culture, in general and the witness's communication style specifically, can help witness and attorney alike more thoroughly understand where the witness's communication style and the cultural context of the courtroom may not mesh. With that understanding, you can develop a more fruitful relationship between the two of you.

Questions to Ask Yourself

- What is my witness's cultural or social background?

- What are the communicative values associated with my witness's background?

- What communicative style has helped my witness be successful in the past?

- How does my witness's past communicative success style help or hinder effective testimony?

- Have I had a direct conversation with my witness about her communicative culture, values, and learned success?

4.6   Recognize Juror Mistrust in an Unreliable Witness

What do you do when your star witness is someone you know jurors will not find credible, no matter what you do? I was involved in such a situation with a commercial civil trial involving the underlying criminal case of a long-running Ponzi scheme. The criminal trial had taken place, and the perpetrator, who I will call "Joe," was tucked away in a federal prison. The plaintiffs were the scheme's victims. They were pension funds and other sophisticated investors who had lost millions of dollars. The defendant was the bank whose accounts Joe used to perpetrate his scheme. The defendant bank was accused of allowing the scheme to happen, turning a blind eye to the suspicious movement of large amounts of money through its accounts. I was working with the investor plaintiffs.

Who was our star witness? It was Joe, the scheme's perpetrator, of course! He gave his testimony in court, wearing full prison inmate attire, complete with orange jumpsuit and handcuffs. After all, it was he who could best provide the testimony about what the bank managers were told and what they did in response. He was the one who told them. He was the one who benefited from their response. His story essentially was one of being granted complete freedom to use his bank accounts without alarms being raised about the suspicious nature of his transactions.

The key is to give jurors permission not to believe the incredible person point blank. Instead, you have to build enough support around the content of the testimony so that it can stand in the absence of the credibility of its messenger.

One thing was clear, though: there was no way jurors were going to take Joe's word for it. He was the true culprit and, historically, a very good liar. He defrauded some very sophisticated people. Therefore, we had a dilemma. We had to come up with a plan to bolster the credibility of the *content* of Joe's testimony, despite the fact that there was nothing we could do about perceptions of his character.

So what can be done? Fortunately, there are ways to deal with situations like this one. The key is to give jurors permission not to believe the incredible *person* point blank. Instead, you have to build enough support around the content of the testimony so that it can stand in the absence of the credibility of its messenger.

Jurors do not want to be schemed by the schemer and will protect themselves accordingly. Therefore, your job is to focus on the evidence that corroborates a troublesome witnesses' testimony. The suspect testimony can then stand on the foundation of that other evidence. Jurors don't have to believe a witness if they feel uncomfortable taking the word of an unreliable person. But they can believe the corroborating stories.

In other words, it is important to frame the unreliable witness's testimony in the context of other evidence that supports it. Since, thematically, actions speak louder than words, focus on the actions of others in building a case rather than relying exclusively, or even primarily, on the troublesome witness. Specifically, look for:

1. *consensus* when the information is coming from multiple sources;

2. *consistency* where information, behavior, and testimony seem connected both in and out of the courtroom; and

3. *distinctiveness* when highlighting what is unique or abnormal about the opposition's actions compared to what is standard or normal in similar situations.

Consensus shows us the power of numbers. Not only is information more reliable when coming from multiple sources, but it also gains the power of repetition. People tend to believe what they hear more often.

Scott Hawkins and Steven Hoch (1992) conducted an experiment on how repetition had an impact on the perceived credibility of a statement.[5] They found that their research subjects rated consumer trivia statements as more truthful when they have been exposed to those statements multiple times. It is interesting to contrast this research with that of George Belch, who found that cognitive responses toward advertisements grew increasingly *negative* as the repeated exposure to the same commercial within a one-hour television program increased.[6]

In light of these two studies, how can you reap the benefits of repetition without overplaying the message to your detriment? The answer is consensus: have it come from multiple sources and different vantage points.

An illustration of balancing the benefit of repetition with the danger of irritating people comes from the field of advertising, where repeated messages abound. Research like that cited above is the foundation behind advertising campaigns that use tag lines repeated by different spokespeople. It has the benefit of the repetition, but without the risk of losing credibility by having that message recur from the same source. The famous "Got milk?" campaign that began in 1993 is an example of a successful strategy that used the repeated consensus of famous and impactful people to send a message, increasing the perception of the truthfulness of that message. "Milk. It does a body good."

In most trials, needless to say, consensus does not come from high-powered celebrities in catchy commercials, but you can apply the concepts to the testimony gleaned from the characters of the case.

---

5. Scott A. Hawkins & Steven J. Hoch, *Low-Involvement Learning: Memory without Evaluation*, 19 Journal of Consumer Research 212 (1992).

6. George E. Belch, *The Effects of Television Commercial Repetition on Cognitive Response and Message Acceptance*, 9 Journal of Consumer Research 56 (1982).

National Institute for Trial Advocacy

The concept of *consistency* further advances that consensus beyond the words of witnesses. Consistency is using information, evidence, and the behavior to further illustrate the message we want to relay. It is more consensus, but in a different form, using actions and not just words

So for the "Got Milk" campaign, while the different celebrities provided consensus, the choice of using athletes and known, healthy celebrities provided a consistency of that healthy image. It is not just about preaching, but about illustrating that the message is also being practiced.

With consensus and consistency on your side, *distinctiveness* becomes an important contrast. This is about leaving the opposition as the "odd man out." Show that the other party's actions in the case go against the flow of what is normal in the field of practice. Even without a hard set of rules or standards, evidence of common and accepted practices can further strengthen your position and support witness testimony: show the contrast between what they did and what others do.

If jurors see the testimony from an incredible witness as something that connects the dots of the consensus of other witnesses and the consistency of evidence, not as the evidence itself, they feel more comfortable accepting the information. Odds are, once jurors perceive that a witness's story is backed up by information that paints a consistent picture, they will be more willing to open themselves to believing the witness's story as a whole—without having to admit that they have done so.

If jurors see the testimony from an incredible witness as something that connects the dots of the consensus of other witnesses and the consistency of evidence, not as the evidence itself, they feel more comfortable accepting the information.

In the Ponzi scheme trial, the trial team was able to establish a body of testimonial evidence that showed *consensus* supporting Joe's story about his dealings with the defendant's bank and his understanding that the institution's managers were able to see the movement of large amounts of money. Some of that consensus came from the defendant bank's personnel themselves. We showed *consistency* in the bank management's behavior, using documents and bank records that illustrated examples of transactions involving large amounts of cash that the managers did not investigate or question. Finally, we used experts from other banks to illustrate what the standard industry practices were for banks at the time, highlighting the *distinctiveness* of the bank's behavior. The strategy worked. Verdict for the plaintiffs. And the jurors still found Joe a despicable character.

Questions to Ask Yourself

- Is my witness untrustworthy?

- Can I show consensus among other witnesses to support what my witness says?

- What evidence do I have to illustrate consistency between my witness's testimony and the case facts?

- Can I support my witness's testimony by showing a contrast between the opposition's actions and what is "normal?"

- Does my body of evidence supporting my witness's testimony give jurors an out, so they do not have to rely on my bad witness?

4.7   Deal with Adverse Witnesses Strategically

In a Las Vegas case, a defendant nephrologist was accused of failing to appropriately monitor the correction of the mineral levels in a patient's blood, which had been depleted by excessive alcohol consumption to a dangerous, life-threatening level. The claim was that as a result of the doctor correcting the levels too quickly, the patient, instead of having a massive hangover, was left with permanent and severe neurological deficits.

The dilemma for the plaintiff's counsel was whether to call the defendant doctor as an adverse witness in its case. The decision to call the doctor would give the plaintiff a chance to present the defendant first in an adversarial context, hitting the target issues hard and quickly, and letting the jurors form a negative first impression for the doctor. This was a fine strategy.

The decision not to call the doctor would provide the jurors the chance to hear the case facts void of the doctor's input. Even if the jurors eventually found the defendant credible, this would eliminate the risk of adverse examination backfiring and causing the jurors to form a favorable impression of the defendant during the plaintiff's case. This also was a fine strategy.

In this case, the plaintiff decided to call the doctor adversely. Now the defendant had a dilemma. In this trial venue, defense counsel could perform the entire direct examination during the plaintiff's case after the adverse examination, or it could solely do some quick rehabilitation on key issues and then call the doctor again for full direct during the defense's own case.

If the defense were to perform the full direct examination of the witness during the opposing case, it could stop the plaintiff's momentum and interject defense themes, immediately presenting a better image of the defendant and his messages early. The full direct examination after adverse examination would also deny the plaintiff a "second bite" at cross-examination. The defendant would be on the stand only once.

Moreover, for a troubling witness, performing the entire direct examination during the plaintiff's case would reap the benefit of a phenomenon studied in the field of learning psychology—retroactive interference. This is a phenomenon in which new information interferes with and inhibits recall of information that had been learned previously. Retroactive interference, now widely accepted as a basic tenet of learning psychology, was discovered by German experimental psychologist Georg Elias Müller in the late 1800s.[7]

In one of Müller's experiments, he and one of his students presented study participants with a list of syllables for six minutes. The participants were split

---

7. Georg E. Müller & A. Pilzecker, *Experimentelle Beiträge zur Lehre von Gedächtnis*, 1 ZEITSCHRIFT FÜR PSYCHOLOGIE 1 (1900).

into two groups and tested on how many syllables they remembered from the list. In the experimental group, in between being presented with the syllables and being asked to recall them, they were shown three landscape paintings and were asked to describe them. The second group was not shown the paintings. Not surprisingly, the participants who were not shown the paintings recalled more syllables than the participants who were. The new information interfered with or blocked the prior learning.

Similarly, in trial, retroactive interference may increase the chance that subsequent case information may block jurors' recollection of the troubling aspects of a problematic witness. Presenting the entirety of the testimony during the plaintiff's case gives the defense the benefit of retroactive interference with the hope that the rest of the trial proceedings will dilute some of the memories of the doctor's communicative shortcomings.

So, for the defense, conducting the full examination of a defendant during plaintiff's case is a fine strategy.

If, however, the defense were to decide to wait and call the defendant for direct examination during its own presentation of evidence, defense counsel would reap the benefit of hearing all of the plaintiff witnesses, enabling her to more fully address the entirety of the opposing testimony during direct examination. It would also give more air time to a likable defendant. This is also a fine strategy.

In trials, however, we must evaluate the strategy for each case afresh. While one strategy can be fine in one case with one witness, it can and will backfire with another.

While there are certainly benefits and pitfalls with each strategic choice, the real issue is that I have seen attorneys choose a strategy and use it in every case. It brings up the "status quo" bias studied by William Samuelson and Richard Zeckhauser in 1988.[8] The two researchers found that people hold a strong bias toward maintaining a decision already in place instead of making changes, even when the decision involves important issues. It is the reason why incumbent politicians have the advantage over their adversaries in elections. We are drawn toward the familiar.

In trials, however, we must evaluate the strategy for each case afresh. While one strategy can be fine in one case with one witness, it can and will backfire with another.

So, let's go back to the nephrology trial. The defendant doctor was the kind of person who was very intelligent and literal in his work. He was a good doctor. On the other hand, he was a terrible communicator because of both his personality

---

8. William Samuelson & Richard Zeckhauser, *Status Quo Bias in Decision-Making*, 1 JOURNAL OF RISK AND UNCERTAINTY 7 (1988).

and cultural communication style, which made him prone to unhelpful utterances. He was too deferential to opposing counsel and failed to advocate for himself.

As stated before, the plaintiff called the doctor adversely to give the jurors the negative first impression he was sure to provide. The defense, in response, decided to rip the Band-Aid off, stop the plaintiff's momentum short, and examine the doctor fully after the adverse examination, during plaintiff's case. Counsel introduced the defense themes, rehabilitated the doctor's image as much as possible early on, and did not present the doctor again during the duration of a several-week trial. The idea was that jurors' memory of his communicative issues would fade over weeks of trial and testimony. Given a witness with cultural barriers to communication and difficulty testifying, both sides made the right decision based on this particular case and this particular defendant.

In a different case, however, with a defendant who communicates well, whether a doctor or a manager or a delivery truck driver, the plaintiff may be doing his own case a disservice by calling a defendant adversely who may be likable or sympathetic to a jury. In this instance, it is plaintiff who is giving the defense two bites at the apple—presenting a witness who will be well received twice during the trial: in both the plaintiff's case and the defense's. I have seen likable defendants presented as both the first and last witness in a trial. The strength of the witness and his ability to bookend the evidence was a great asset to the defense.

Getting too comfortable with a mode of how to handle these situations can be dangerous. First, for the litigator who goes to trial frequently, having a set formula will mean that opposing counsel knows what to expect. Second, while a strategy may work in a case today, it can be detrimental in the one you have next month. There are too many idiosyncratic factors to consider in each case for it to be wise to use the same strategy every time.

You must consider not only the length of trial and the resulting tendency for jurors' memories to fade, but the likability of a witness or potential for that witness to be sympathetic as well. In cases where a defense witness is important enough to potentially be called adversely, she is important enough for counsel to critically examine how to go about calling her.

Questions to Ask Yourself

- Do I deal with adverse witnesses the same way for every case?

- How effective a witness is at issue?

- Is my case in a better position if jurors' memories of her are blocked by time and subsequent information?

- Is my case in a better position if this witness is presented multiple times and at different points in the trial or just once?

- (*for defendants*) Does the court allow me to perform my entire direct examination of my witness when that witness was called adversely by the opposition?

4.8   Know the Real Power of Impeaching

Back in 2007, some of my colleagues and I had a question: when an attorney impeaches a witness with a prior inconsistent statement, has the credibility of that witness been totally eviscerated?

We knew that many people in the litigation world thought that was the case. We weren't so sure. So we did what researchers do—we collected data. In our study, we gave 808 jury-eligible adults from across the country a six-item questionnaire. The questionnaire addressed how those jurors would respond to a witness's statement on the stand that is inconsistent with what the witness said at a prior time. The questionnaire items were as follows:

> Please answer the following questions considering witness testimony in a civil trial (when one party sues another party seeking money in damages), and not a criminal trial (when the government brings charges against an individual for alleged criminal misconduct).

1. If a witness in a trial says something in court that is different from what was said in earlier statements, that witness is more likely:

   a. Purposely lying on the stand

   b. Making an honest mistake

2. If a witness's testimony on the stand conflicts with his/her pervious statement, I would most likely:

   a. Believe what the witness said in the previous statement

   b. Believe what the witness is saying on the stand

   c. Focus on how the witness behaves (body language, etc.) to determine whether or not he/she is telling the truth on the stand

   d. Disregard everything the witness has said

3. The stress of giving testimony in a legal proceeding likely causes witnesses to make honest mistakes in their testimony

   a. Strongly Disagree

   b. Somewhat Disagree

   c. Completely Uncertain

   d. Somewhat Agree

   e. Strongly Agree

4. Events that lead to a lawsuit are so remarkable that I have a hard time believing that witnesses would forget them, no matter how much time had passed

   a. Strongly Disagree

   b. Somewhat Disagree

   c. Completely Uncertain

   d. Somewhat Agree

   e. Strongly Agree

5. In general, while testifying under oath in a civil trial, most people:

   a. Will say anything to keep themselves out of trouble

   b. Will be as honest as possible

6. If a witness says something on the stand that is inconsistent with his/her previous statement, none of that witness's testimony can be believed, regardless of the circumstances.

   a. Strongly Disagree

   b. Somewhat Disagree

   c. Completely Uncertain

   d. Somewhat Agree

   e. Strongly Agree

The results of our research were published in Defense Research Institute's (DRI) publication, *For the Defense*. We called the article, "Impeaching with Prior Inconsistent Statements: It's Not as Devastating as You Might Think."[9] The title gives you an indication of what we found.

The results were that most jurors (72 percent) tend to believe that witnesses are generally honest. While most (60 percent) would also believe that a witness who says something in court that was different than a prior statement is purposely lying, only a small proportion (20 percent) said that they would disregard everything the witness said in that instance.

Instead, the majority of the jurors who took the survey (64 percent) indicated that when faced with a witness who made a prior inconsistent statement, they would focus on how the witness behaves to determine whether or not she is telling the truth on the stand.

---

9. Richard G. Stuhan, Melissa M. Gomez & Daniel Wolfe, *Impeaching with Prior Inconsistent Statements: It's Not as Devastating as You Might Think—An Original Study*, 14 FOR THE DEFENSE 14 (2007).

The punch line is this: impeaching with prior inconsistent statements is obviously helpful in damaging a witness's credibility, but is not always the slam dunk we may think it is. Instead, jurors are typically willing to consider that human factors such as anxiety associated with giving testimony in court (59 percent) and the tendency of memories to fade as time passes (46 percent) can lead a witness to making honest mistakes.

Impeaching with prior inconsistent statements is obviously helpful in damaging a witness's credibility, but is not always the slam dunk we may think it is.

In an automotive accident case in the South, the driver of a tractor trailer was involved in a collision that left his truck disabled on a rural highway in the early hours of a dark morning. Another motorist in a small personal vehicle did not see the truck in the dark roadway and hit the truck. The motorist was killed. There were inconsistencies in the truck driver's account of events in the moments leading up to the initial accident that left his vehicle disabled. In the report that he gave the police, he questioned whether he fell asleep, but in deposition testimony he denied falling asleep, stating that his memory of those moments had come back to him.

I was helping to defend the driver, and concerned about the credibility of his re-appearing memory, we presented the case to a mock jury and asked them how they perceived his inconsistencies. What we learned was that, while there were criticisms of the driver, his testimony's inconsistency was not one of the most pressing ones. Instead, the jurors believed that with the trauma of the accident and the passage of time, it was understandable that his memory may not be quite clear. One of our panelists laughed, stating, "That guy didn't know what was upside down or right side up when this was happening. We can't worry about what he said." His comment was greeted with agreement around the table. Therefore, the jurors dismissed the driver's memory of the moments before the accident and focused their decisions on other evidence.

There are two key considerations regarding inconsistent statements: one for when you are the questioner, and one for when your witness is the one being questioned. First, when you impeach a witness with a prior inconsistent statement on cross-examination, unless the witness has turned into a babbling mess on the stand and can't recover, the witness has not necessarily lost credibility. Relying on one or two impeachments, no matter how devastating they may seem to the other side, can leave you open to the possibility that jurors will forgive those witnesses. Never get complacent or overconfident.

The second relates to your own witnesses. This is not to say that you should dismiss inconsistent statements as irrelevant. It is still important to avoid them by making sure a witness: 1) gives truthful testimony from the beginning (which is the easiest and most important way to stay consistent), and 2) is well-versed on the prior statements he has given before trial.

But impeachments can happen, even with truthful witnesses who studied their prior statements. Therefore, when preparing your witness, you must coach him on how to handle such impeachment situations with poise so he does not become that babbling mess on the stand. He is more likely to be forgiven if he handles the situation well.

When preparing your witness, you must coach him on how to handle such impeachment situations with poise so he does not become that babbling mess on the stand.

It is clear that jurors attend to a witness's behavioral, nonverbal cues as much as, if not more than, the content of that witness's testimony. Those cues are especially critical when the witness is confronted with their inconsistent statement. Someone who becomes the proverbial "deer in headlights" is more likely to be thought as a person caught in a lie. On the other hand, someone who takes a breath, looks the jurors/examiner square in the eye and says, "What I meant when I said that was . . ." or "After taking another look at the documents, I realize I was incorrect . . ." has a much better chance of jurors considering the witness a human being and not a liar.

Of course, there are limits to the extent to which jurors will accept inconsistencies regardless of how confident the witness is. Take a case in Iowa in which a cardiothoracic surgeon was accused of botching a heart surgery, requiring the plaintiff to have a total heart replacement. The plaintiff's medical negligence expert changed his opinion three times during the course of the litigation. Each time he came up with a theory of why the defendant surgeon was negligent, the evidence contradicted that theory. So he changed it. Three times. By the time we got to trial, defense counsel led the expert through the timeline of his changing opinions. Was the expert confident and prepared in his responses? Yes. But in this case, his demeanor wasn't going to help him. His credibility was eviscerated.

Questions to Ask Yourself

- Has a witness been impeached with an inconsistent statement?

- How did the witness react nonverbally to being impeached?

- Do I put too much emphasis on the power of one inconsistent statement?

4.9   Accept that Your Witness May Not Be Likable

In a small county in Georgia, there was a case involving a man who received third-degree burns all over his body after an explosion in the plant where he was working. His face was disfigured. He had been burned so badly, he lost parts of his hands. He had every reason to be a miserable, angry person after what happened to him. But he wasn't. He was a fighter. He spoke with hope and courage, not despair. He was a hometown hero. He was an inspiration to the community. He was the plaintiff in a case against my client, a company that inspected the equipment involved in the explosion.

We were in trouble. Our defenses were very technical. The plaintiff's injuries were the stuff of nightmares. The plaintiff himself was one of the most likable people I had ever encountered in a lawsuit. I cannot express the relief I felt when I received the call that we were able to resolve the case before it got to a jury.

Having a likable witness definitely helps. In some cases it can make or break a case. But let's face it, clients who are hometown heroes or inspirations to their community are rare finds.

I tell this story to make it very clear: having a likable witness definitely helps. In some cases it can make or break a case. But let's face it, clients who are hometown heroes or inspirations to their community are rare finds.

In some respects, we have either overstated the importance of witnesses being likable or we have developed too narrow a definition of *how* a witness should be liked. In most instances, it is true that jurors will find it easier to believe and find in favor of someone they like. Sometimes, though, you may be faced with a client or a witness who is just not going to relate well to the Average Joe. Trying to use witness preparation tactics to force such a person to be "likable" or to behave in a manner inconsistent with her core personality will not only fail, but will most likely make her appear dishonest. Because it is dishonest.

The first question to ask is: what does likability mean? Expert witness and writer William Cottringer performed a simple, informal experiment in 2002 in which he asked a broad sample of people to tell him the top five things that influence them in seeing another person as "likable" and the top five that make a person "unlikable." He subsequently wrote an article called "The Power of Likability" based on what he learned about what makes a person likable, and developed ten traits that had the most influence on likability.[10] I found his results intriguing. He advises:

- be honest;

---

10. William S. Cottringer, *The Power of Likability*, http://www.authorsden.com/visit/viewArticle. asp?id=6874 (last visited Jan. 26, 2016).

- be humble;

- learn empathy;

- laugh often;

- be positive;

- control hostility;

- be polite;

- act smart (intelligent);

- appear attractive (in terms of proper grooming and hygiene);

- listen more.

Obviously, laughter often is not congruent with the courtroom context, but the other traits certainly make sense when considering what jurors will find as favorable characteristics of a witness on the stand. Let's face it, though, there are some people who simply can't pull all (or even some) of these strategies off.

I remember a contentious contract dispute case between two companies in Los Angeles. I was working with the plaintiff company in the dispute. Our key witness was the CEO. He was a wealthy, successful businessman. He was not humble. He was not empathetic. He was not positive or encouraging. He was the kind of guy people didn't like. But he was the kind of leader people respected. He was excellent at running a business. He was not excellent at relating to people.

For a witness like this, the critical component of witness preparation was not trying to transform him into a warm and fuzzy person. Instead, the critical component was to leave jurors with the impression that if you had a serious business to run, he was the one you wanted to run it. He dotted his i's and crossed his t's. While not very likable, he was intelligent, thorough, tough, and most of all, honest.

For this witness, honesty wasn't just reflected in the testimony he gave about the contract dealings at issue in the case, but it was also reflected in being honest about who he was as a person. In fact, the trial team took underscoring who the witness was a step further. Even the board members of the company admitted on the stand that the witness was not the easiest personality to deal with—but, boy, did he know how to run a business with integrity.

Your witness needs to realize that her behavior in the courtroom is the only information jurors will have about how she behaves outside of the courtroom. So what she wants jurors to believe about her character and behavior related to the case, she needs to demonstrate at trial.

This is absolutely not to suggest it is OK to forego behavioral work with witnesses when they are not the kind of folks who will win jurors' hearts. Instead, it is to say that having the right focus in witness preparation is critical. Your witness needs to realize that her behavior in the courtroom is the only information jurors will have about how she behaves outside of the courtroom. So what she wants jurors to believe about her character and behavior related to the case, she needs to demonstrate at trial.

Regarding the contract case, in terms of Cottringer's factors, we understood that working to make the CEO positive, empathetic, or humble was an exercise in futility. But we could demonstrate his honesty, ability to control hostility, and willingness to listen. Some is better than none.

The reason why we worked on those variables as opposed to others was because they were critical to the big-picture message of the case even if they did not make him particularly likable. Those variables had to do with our witness's willingness to hear, understand, and respect the process before him. If the CEO did not demonstrate respect for the rules of the courtroom (as some high-powered business people tend to do with a "my way or the highway" disposition), jurors would have likely perceived him as someone who did not follow the rules in business. Likable or not, *that* would have been detrimental to his case. Preparation for this witness focused on thwarting any courtroom behavior that would reflect an image congruent with that of the person who thinks he is too important to follow the rules of fair business dealings opposing counsel was arguing.

Specifically, our witness needed to show that he knew how to play by the rules by answering the questions asked without talking through or over people; by addressing the court with respect; and by being forthcoming, straightforward, clear, and concise. No warm fuzzies needed. He did all of those things. The jurors noticed. As predicted, the jurors we interviewed after the trial told us that they didn't like our witness personally, but they believed that he was a good businessman who followed the rules of fair business dealings. He won their respect and their verdict. They liked him in the manner they needed to like him.

So the point is this: all the witness preparation in the world can't make a person into something he isn't. If you try, jurors will see right through it. What is important, however, is that you understand the strength of who your witness *is*, and focus your preparation efforts work on highlighting an image of your witness that is consistent with and bolsters the case story. It is critical to understand and remove the barriers to likeability if you can; otherwise, you have to let a duck be a duck.

Questions to Ask Yourself

- Do I have a likable witness?

- What image messages about my witness do the jurors need to receive to believe my witness's story?

- Does that image message include likability?

- Am I trying to make my witness likable in a manner that is inconsistent with who my witness is?

- If my witness cannot be likable, how can I effectively account for that in my presentation of the case?

PART FIVE

MAINTAINING THE RIGHT CASE IMAGE

5.1   Never Underestimate the Power of Just Being Nice

Picture this: Bucks County, Pennsylvania. It is sometime in the late '80s. I am sitting in a dingy classroom somewhere within the halls of Council Rock High School. Hair: Big. Eyeliner: Electric blue. This class is my first introduction to psychology, the field that will become my future. My teacher, Mr. Curran, tall, lanky, and still holding on to the fashion sensibilities of the sixties, writes on the chalkboard in large, block letters: "NEVER UNDERESTIMATE THE POWER OF JUST BEING NICE." Then he sits down and lets the students marinate for a while in the statement. Silently.

I have seen many litigators make the error of believing that to zealously advocate for their clients, they need to be vicious to the witnesses on the other side. What I want to tell you is that this tactic, in general, does not work in front of a jury.

Decades later, I still regularly reflect on his words and their applicability to all contexts of the human experience.

So what does being nice have to do with jury trials? In my humble opinion, a great deal. I have seen many litigators make the error of believing that to zealously advocate for their clients, they need to be vicious to the witnesses on the other side. What I want to tell you is that this tactic, in general, does not work in front of a jury. After all, you catch more flies with honey than vinegar, right?

Of course, being nice does not mean that you fail to make strong arguments or expose bad behavior. It does mean, however, that you can attack behavior without attacking the individual. I have seen people brutally and personally attacked on the stand. I have seen litigants being called "cheats" and "liars" by counsel. Jurors don't like that. It is a rare situation when it is warranted. No matter how despicable the behavior was, once the attack gets personal, the attorney looks bad, not the witness.

I have seen jurors vehemently come to the defense of witnesses they perceive as being attacked. Taking a look at how we are wired, it makes sense. Sympathy and empathy are inherent in the human DNA. In fact, Romero, Castellanos, and de Waal linked this primitive response to chimpanzees.[1] They specifically found that chimpanzees consoled other chimpanzees who they had seen been attacked by offering physical contact as comfort. In other words, feeling sympathetic concern toward someone being attacked is not a higher level of functioning. It is primitive. It is ingrained.

In a contract dispute trial, opposing counsel was cross-examining one of our expert witnesses. Counsel was yelling. He was flailing. He was angry. Our witness tried to stay calm and answer the questions, but was obviously shaken by the tone of the questioning.

During interviews we conducted after the trial, the jurors stated that they did not remember much about the content of that cross-examination. What they remembered was the attorney's show and how they felt about it. It reminded me of something poet Maya Angelou said: "I've learned that people will forget what you said, people will forget what you did, but people will never forget how you made them feel."

The jurors relayed that they felt bad that this witness was forced to put up with such an attack. In essence, while opposing counsel was trying to make the witness look nervous about the content of his testimony, he only succeeded in making the witness look upset about being verbally abused. In turn, the jurors were upset. The jurors turned that upset to anger against the very attorney who was using those tactics to get them on his side.

I have observed many cases, and I have yet to find a situation in which it is necessary or appropriate to launch a full frontal attack on another human being. Attorneys should attack decisions, point out prior inconsistent statements, question behaviors, and do so in a challenging, yet poised and professional manner. There is an art to crushing a witness's credibility without appearing like a tyrant or bully. If you employ that art, jurors will more likely perceive the confrontation as warranted and professional instead of an ill-tempered attack. You will appear more in control and confident, making jurors pay attention to your points and not your volume.

There is an art to crushing a witness's credibility without appearing like a tyrant or bully.

It is important to note that this advice doesn't mean you should be soft spoken. It doesn't mean backing down. It means being aware of crossing the line to what

---

1. T. Romero, M. A. Castellanos & F. B. M. de Waal, *Consolation as Possible Expression of Sympathetic Concern Among Chimpanzees*, 107 PROCEEDINGS OF THE NATIONAL ACADEMY OF SCIENCES OF THE UNITED STATES OF AMERICA 12110 (2010).

National Institute for Trial Advocacy

jurors may perceive as unnecessary abuse. If the cross-examination needs to get heated, it needs to get heated. But you have to earn the right to get heated in the jurors' eyes by showing that the witness deserves a more assertive challenge before launching that challenge.

Of course, it doesn't hurt that jurors will find it much easier to like you if they perceive you as a nice person. Even if in the battle of the trial you can't quite achieve "nice," it is possible to come away avoiding being perceived as quite something else.

Questions to Ask Yourself

- Have I earned the right to become more aggressive in front of my jurors?

- In my presentation, am I attacking the witness's character or the witness's actions?

- Is the manner in which I am presenting run the risk of having jurors feel the need to defend an unfairly abused witness?

- What messages do my tone and nonverbal behaviors send to the jurors?

5.2   Recognize the Reality of Home-Field Advantage

Jeremy Jamieson from Northeastern University (2010) conducted a meta-analysis of sports-outcome data to examine the impact of home-field advantage on the likelihood of winning athletic events.[2] He found that overall, the home team is expected to win 60 percent of all athletic contests. Does the same apply in jury trials? Unfortunately, this question requires the answer most unpopular when given by any consultant. That answer is, of course: it depends.

First, it depends on the venue. Some places really are more about the home team than others. Take Pittsburgh, Pennsylvania. It is a home-field advantage kind of place. From both the real and mock trials I have experienced there, it is clear that while jurors are generally reasonable and thoughtful, there is an underlying sense of pride in the accomplishments of homegrown businesses and hometown folks. An outside party coming to criticize that which is homegrown clearly has a steeper incline to climb than a party from the home turf. That is not to say that the mountain is insurmountable. The trek is simply steeper.

What matters more is how well the trial team and client show respect for the cultural values of a venue through their interaction in the courtroom.

Other places, such as New York City, may have less of an inclination to support the home team. There are so many people and businesses that originate from other places that the sense of pride in the "homegrown" gets diluted there because the roots of the venue tend toward the planted, not the indigenous.

What matters more is how well the trial team and client show respect for the cultural values of a venue through their interaction in the courtroom.

The question of juror preference for what is "local" reminds me of a product liability case in Boston, for which I was working with the defense. The lead attorney for the plaintiffs was from Texas. He had a heavy, unmistakable southern drawl. Throughout the trial, he kept a quiet seat next to the local attorney, who sported the clear local accent. It was obvious that the plaintiffs wanted to be perceived as hometown and were afraid that such an obvious indication of having an "outsider" at their table would be problematic for their case. The lawyer from Texas, who was actually much better versed in the case and the accusations against the product's manufacturer, than the local attorney who presented the case, didn't say a word during the entire trial. Not one word. Was it the right call? I can't say, but the defense prevailed, so maybe it wasn't.

---

2. Jeremy Jamieson, *The Home Field Advantage in Athletics: A Meta-Analysis*, 40 Journal of Applied Social Psychology 1819 (2010).

National Institute for Trial Advocacy

In my practice, I have found that being the attorney from the outside doesn't mean you need to keep your mouth shut. It does, however, mean you have to do your homework to *understand and appreciate* the people of the venue. This is different than needing to be one of them. You do not need to change who you are or who your client is. In fact, trying too hard to fit in is transparent and appears dishonest. Texas jurors will notice that those cowboy boots that attorney from up north is wearing are fresh from the box and will believe that attorney is trying to artificially ingratiate himself to the jurors. Because he is. And, yes, that actually happened.

I recall another instance in which a Colorado attorney was in a trial against my client in West Virginia. The judge in that trial kept two large Styrofoam cups on the bench throughout trial. One was his coffee. The other his spittoon. We were definitely in West Virginia.

Concerned about wanting to be seen as local, this young trial lawyer brought his father, who lived locally, to the trial and introduced him to the court and to the jurors. That went over like a lead balloon with both the jurors and our tobacco-chewing judge.

On the other hand, not trying hard enough to modify your approach to reflect and respect the cultural values of the venue will not bode well either. For example, you may get away with a more confrontational cross-examination in New York City, where a higher level of assertiveness is expected, than in Savannah, Georgia, where politeness is valued as a part of Southern culture. Again, the line you must walk is one of respecting the local culture, not pretending to be a part of it. If walked well, an out-of-towner can be as well received as a local.

Of course, there are some cases that simply will not be well received if they fly in the face of the values of a venue, whether counsel is local or otherwise. Take the case of a woman suing the mascot for the Philadelphia Phillies baseball team, the Phillie Phanatic. She claimed that the Phanatic injured her while engaging in silly antics to entertain the crowd. The trial was to take place in Philadelphia. The plaintiff's attorney called me to ask for assistance. My initial reaction was this: "You are suing the Phillie Phanatic in Philadelphia. Philadelphia loves the Phillie Phanatic. Your chances of a win on this are not good." So to test my theory, we conducted a telephone survey to assess just how much people in Philadelphia loved their Phanatic and what their visceral reaction would be to accusations that his silly antics hurt someone. The results were as follows: "Philadelphia loves the Phillie Phanatic. Leave our Phanatic alone." So because the Phanatic refused to accept a settlement offer—he clearly was well aware of how much he was loved in Philadelphia—this client was forced to take the case to trial. Plaintiff lost. No surprise to anyone. She didn't have a chance.

Understanding a venue is about both respecting the court's procedures and understanding the community values well enough to know what will fly and what will clash. When in Rome, you don't have to do what the Romans do. You just have to know what they do and show respect for it while you do what you do.

The fact is, in any venue, whether in your hometown or across the country, a strategy that is palatable and understandable to the people within the community will win a case, regardless of whether you are from the same town or not.

When in Rome, you don't have to do what the Romans do.
You just have to know what they do and show respect for it while
you do what you do.

In the end, regardless of where the game is played, the most important predictor of who will win is who has the better game strategy and the most prepared team.

Questions to Ask Yourself

- Does the population of trial venue lean toward more transplanted people or indigenous?

- What are the cultural values of my trial venue?

- Is there anything about my case that will clash with the cultural values of my trial venue?

- How do I show respect for the cultural values in my trial venue?

- Does the manner I am trying to show respect for my trial venue appear sincere or contrived?

5.3   Investigate Public Opinion

I was once interviewed by a local news station about a trial that was pending in Pennsylvania. The defendant was Oprah Winfrey. You know, the media megastar and arguably one of the most influential women in America. The topic was whether Winfrey could get a fair trial in Philadelphia considering that just about every potential juror would know who she is.

My short answer to the reporters was this: simply being familiar with a celebrity, a company, or topic does not make a person biased either for or against him, her, or it. Just because the court would have been challenged to find one person (let alone twelve) unfamiliar with Oprah Winfrey, that familiarity does not necessarily equate to bias. Actually, I may be more concerned about a person who has not heard of her. Where has that person been for the past thirty years? The questions to a potential panel must probe much deeper than simple familiarity.

The case related to a school for girls that Winfrey founded in Africa in a philanthropic effort to strengthen the knowledge and professional development of the women of Africa's future. Who doesn't love that? Unfortunately, there were substantiated allegations that some of the school faculty and staff had taken this effort as an opportunity to sexually abuse students. They victimized the very children Winfrey intended to strengthen.

When the media revealed that this had happened, Winfrey released statements and granted interviews to express her dismay. She specifically named and voiced her disappointment with a woman she had appointed the head of the school—a woman from Philadelphia. The head of the school was not one of the abusers, but the tone and content of Winfrey's comments were such that she believed this person failed to protect the children. The abuse occurred on her watch.

The head of school, in turn, sued Winfrey for defamation, asserting that those public statements made it impossible for her to find another job. After all, who would hire a person who failed the beloved Oprah Winfrey?

The issue for this case was that it dealt with a high-profile celebrity in a highly publicized defamation trial about the highly publicized (and highly emotionally charged) topic of abuse at a highly publicized school. The layers of relevant public opinion here ran much deeper than Winfrey herself.

Similarly, there are other examples of high-profile cases that struggled with finding a fair and impartial jury. Take the criminal cases of George Zimmerman, Casey Anthony, and Jerry Sandusky. The media circuses that enveloped these cases were omnipresent.

So what is the real challenge in these instances? At the most obvious level, the media attention the cases received certainly wrought havoc with the jury selection process. Like the Winfrey case, it was all but impossible to eliminate all jurors who had heard about the cases, let alone who had some kind of opinion about them.

Regardless, the consideration for the attorneys and the court in these cases is not whether potential jurors have heard about the case; instead, it is about whether those jurors have developed opinions that they will not yield, regardless of the evidence presented in court.

While these cases are extreme examples of how public opinion can influence a high-profile case, these issues are relevant in any kind of case in which public opinion is a factor. A community may have certain perceptions of a public or corporate litigant, an event that received extensive media attention, or other incidents that have been publicized and have similarities to the case at hand. I recall a trucking accident trial that was being held soon after the media hailstorm surrounding a trucking accident that involved a Walmart tractor trailer and actor/comedian Tracy Morgan. Because there was an issue for the driver in the Walmart incident with driving beyond drive-time limits, there was substantial media focus on the issue of tractor-trailer drivers driving while tired, thereby increasing their risk of falling asleep at the wheel of gigantic vehicles. Media-induced national public concern over tired truck drivers did not bode well for a case that involved allegations of my client's driver falling asleep at the wheel. Therefore, it was not a surprise when the Walmart/Morgan incident and a global concern over tired truck drivers was discussed by the jurors during our mock trial deliberations.

Moreover, because of a specific history or culture within a particular community, public perceptions in one community may be different than in others. I recall a contract dispute over a popular television show. The trial team was in New York City, and the trial was in Los Angeles. The trial team asked why we couldn't just do our jury research in New York. "Won't it be easier?" While easier, perceptions of the entertainment community, especially the negotiations behind it, are quite idiosyncratic in Los Angeles, where film and television are the primary industry. That cultural variable could not be duplicated anywhere else regardless of the fact that New York jurors may have been just as familiar with the television program.

The trouble with public opinion is that it seems so public—we think we understand what the opinion is and how it will influence perceptions of a case. That is not always true, and such assumptions cause trouble.

The trouble with public opinion is that it seems so public—we think we understand what the opinion is and how it will influence perceptions of a case. That is not always true, and such assumptions cause trouble. In Atlantic City, New Jersey, the closing of multiple casinos had an indescribable impact on the community. Jobs were being lost, abandoned casinos littered the boardwalk, and homes were going into foreclosure. There was substantial concern from plaintiff and defense attorneys alike about what impact these changes in the Atlantic City economy would have on juror decisions. Would jurors be concerned about awarding damages against a casino for fear of making the situation worse? Would they be so angry that damages against viable casinos would skyrocket?

A good client and friend expressed his concern about these issues, pointing to articles written and local commentary that had been submitted to media publications by some residents. The opinions were strong, but as I told this client, the publications contained the opinion of one or two outspoken people. The vocal few. That voice may or may not represent more widespread opinion. We can't assume that because the opinion is expressed publicly it represents what people are really thinking. It may, but we can't assume.

Let's examine the Oprah Winfrey trial again. Most people immediately assumed that the plaintiff in the case would be in big trouble at trial. After all, just about everyone loves Oprah, right? The news report I participated in also included interviews of community members who were full of praise for Winfrey: "She is an inspiration," "She does so many good things." Therefore, the conclusion was simple: the community would automatically favor the beloved celebrity.

But let's consider the other side. Folks who were openly avid Winfrey fans likely would not be able to participate in the trial—their bias would likely be clear if they answered questions honestly, and they would be struck for cause. Those left may be able to take a more rational approach and perceive the case more through their understanding of the power of Winfrey's voice, even as they considered themselves above that power. Depending on the evidence presented in the case, a perception like that could be quite detrimental to Winfrey's defense.

So, which of these perceptions was more prevalent in the community? What were the characteristics of those who fell on one side or the other? Was there a different perception that was more relevant for this trial? I had no idea. Only the community itself knew. Winfrey settled the case before jury selection began.

It is important to also note that when you focus so much on the high-profile nature of a high-profile case, you may miss some of the other relevant issues that could be at play. Take the George Zimmerman trial from the summer of 2013. Zimmerman was accused of second-degree murder in the shooting death of teenager, Trayvon Martin. Zimmerman admitted to shooting Martin, but claimed that he did so in self-defense. Other hot topics were at play in the case such as gun control, civil rights, and when, if ever, is it right for citizens to use weapons to take neighborhood protection into their own hands. These issues were just as relevant, if not more relevant, to jury selection as the media exposure of the case itself.

When you focus so much on the high-profile nature of a high-profile case, you may miss some of the other relevant issues that could be at play.

Therefore, public opinion and its impact on perceptions of a case are not always predictable, and it is dangerous to assume what the impact is. Look before you leap, especially in cases with high media and monetary exposure. There is no way to know what public opinion really is and how it will impact perceptions of a case without a careful examination.

With a deeper look, you may just find that there is a distinct difference between what you *think* people think, and what they *actually* think.

Questions to Ask Yourself

- What are the high-profile issues that may affect my case?

- Do I have any assumptions about how that issue will affect me case?

- What is the basis for my assumptions? Can I rely on it?

- Are the high-profile issues that may affect my case significant enough to investigate their true impact on perceptions of my case?

5.4 Dress to Impress—Comfortably

How should I dress?

I have been asked this question more than a few times in my career. Once was by a witness who brought no fewer than three suits, five shirts, and four ties to the trial preparation room so I could pick out his clothes for each day of trial. I had another attorney send me pictures of her wearing different outfits so I could advise on the best choice for opening, for cross-examining a witness, or at counsel table. I know that some jury consultants focus heavily on the fashion aspect of image. I, on the other hand, am no Stacy London from TLC's *What Not to Wear* reality show. Therefore, I reviewed the opinions of those with more expertise in the clothing and accessory field before advising clients on how to present the right visual image in a professional context.

The Columbia University Center for Career Education, for example, posts some standard rules for dressing for an interview and creating a professional first impression.[3] The following encapsulates their advice.

Men

Wear a suit in a conservative and dark color, like navy or charcoal, a tie that doesn't draw attention to itself, a pressed shirt (preferably white), and socks that match your pants (never wear white socks).

Women

Wear a pant suit or skirt suit in a conservative color and a conservative blouse. If wearing a skirt suit, make sure the skirt is of a moderate length, and you wear neutral hose without snags or runs. When wearing a dress shirt, women should also button up, taking care to avoid a very revealing neckline.

Shoes

Shoes should be traditional and conservative. They should be in good condition, polished (no scuffmarks), and not run down at the heels. Heels should be a comfortable height and not too high (not more than one to two inches). Avoid wearing open-toed shoes or slingbacks.

Other

- Jewelry and makeup should be discreet. Avoid distracting amounts of both. Generally, men and women should remove their facial piercings if they have them.

---

3. http://www.careereducation.columbia.edu/resources/tipsheets/skills-professional-image (last visited Jan. 26, 2016).

- Pay attention to your grooming. Keep your hair neatly styled and your nails at a professional length. If you wear nail polish, choose a subtle shade and be sure your polish is neat.

- Do not wear perfume, cologne, or fragrance of any kind; your interviewer may be allergic.

- Go over your outfit with a lint brush before the interview.

- When you arrive at your interview, stop by the restroom and give your attire one final check in the mirror.

I definitely have to agree about the facial piercing.

The main concept that Columbia University is trying to relay to its students is that it is good, in general, to be conservative in the way you dress. Although I don't necessarily agree that everyone has to look like a librarian.

Show respect for the courtroom with what you wear.

Instead, based on some of the fashion disasters I have observed in the courtroom, I have developed some of my own ground rules on courtroom image, which may be a little more relaxed than Columbia's strict standards, but still relay the image of professionalism and integrity. These thoughts apply to anyone in the courtroom—attorneys, clients, and witnesses alike. They are as follows.

1. Whether you are litigant or lawyer, show respect for the courtroom with what you wear. The courtroom is a professional setting and should be treated professionally. I once worked on a case in which one of the litigants, seated at opposing counsel's table, showed up to court in jeans. I will admit that this trial involved a dispute about the manufacturing of jeans. Still inappropriate.

2. Ladies, please wear stockings. The no stockings issue is big with me. Yes, even in the summer when you are tan. We are not at the beach. Personally, stockings and I do not get along, so you will not find a skirt suit in my closet. I wear pants. No stockings needed. Some female attorneys believe that it is important to wear skirt suits. If this applies to you, I say go for it. But wear stockings.

   At a trial I attended in Los Angeles, a young, attractive female lawyer on the other side sported bare legs with a relatively short skirt. A male juror was blatantly trying to look up her skirt. He was actually craning his neck to get the best view. I doubt he was taking her seriously.

3. A big question from men is: "to beard or not to beard?" It is best for men to be clean shaven. Some people don't like beards because it hides your face

and makes it harder to read your expression. My only exception is for those men who have had a beard for so long that its absence would be a distraction. A client once told me a story of shaving his beard for a trial, and when his young child saw him, she cried because she didn't recognize him. If it truly is so uncomfortable to lose the beard that you lose focus on the job at hand, trim it close and move on. Otherwise, shave it.

Be aware of drawing too much attention to yourself. You are not the star of the show. Your case is.

---

4. For any gender, if you see the sparkle from ten feet away, leave it home. Big watches, sparkly jewelry, oversized rings, and the like all serve to distract jurors and separate you from them. Jewelry is appropriate as long as it is not too large or flashy. The same goes for bags. If it says "Prada" on it, leave it home.

    I was working on a dental malpractice case in which a patient died after having developing an infection from a tooth pull. The defendant dentist arrived to court with an absolutely gorgeous Prada handbag. Now, I am not the kind of girl who notices or cares much for handbags. But this one was stunningly beautiful. I told our defendant that her bag was fabulous and then made her hide it and never bring it to court again.

5. Beware of clothing that makes you stand out too much. The courtroom is an understated, professional fashion setting. I attended a trial in a Pennsylvania federal court regarding a hedge-fund investment. I was assisting the defendant hedge fund and its manager. One of the corporate representatives for the plaintiff's company was a woman who wore very brightly colored, patterned jackets with coordinating bags each day. While there was nothing wrong with the clothing, per se, she stood out like a sore thumb in the sea of grey and brown suits. A bright color is fine, and is refreshing in a drab, colorless courtroom, but save it for the shirt underneath the suit, not the suit itself. Likewise, nothing is wrong with professionally toned red shoes. But the last thing you want is for jurors to pay more attention to the outfit of the day rather than your case messages.

    The same can apply to men with overly slick suits or outlandish ties. Make sure your suits fit well and feel good, but be careful about appearing overly tailored and expensive.

    Overall, be aware of drawing too much attention to yourself. You are not the star of the show. Your case is.

6. Finally, my most important rule of thumb is that you have to be as comfortable as possible while respecting the professionalism of the courtroom

environment. (Remember the jeans? That was too comfortable). Make sure your clothes fit comfortably, especially if they are new to you or bought specifically for trial. Make sure the neck on your shirt is not too tight. Ties are not supposed to choke you. If you are distracted by your clothing, you are paying attention to clothes and not the case. Again, that is why I choose pant suits. For me, stockings are distractingly uncomfortable. I have to admit, though, I have made clients buy suits despite the fact that they have lived their lives in t-shirts. Those folks just had to deal with a bit of discomfort to look professional.

Questions to Ask Yourself

- Is my appearance professional and respectful to the courtroom?

- Am I comfortable?

- Am I wearing or carrying anything that will distract jurors or alienate them from me?

5.5 Be the Right Reflection of Your Client

With all of the preparations of evidence, witnesses, and trial exhibits, some trial teams fail to address what I consider to be a global truth of jury trials. It is such a simple concept that is all too often ignored. What is it? It is to never forget the following:

At trial, you are a reflection of your client.

No exception.

What does it mean to follow the global truth? In a medical malpractice case, the plaintiffs sued a doctor for failing to diagnose lung cancer, claiming that the doctor ignored the patient's complaints, treated the patient like a number, and didn't care enough to try to understand the nature of the problem. The plaintiff claimed that as a result of a callous and uncaring attitude, the doctor fell below the standard of care in his treatment of the patient. As a result, there was a delay in diagnosis and the cancer became untreatable, leading to the patient's death. The defendant doctor, admittedly, did not have the warmest of personalities, and we worked to help him demonstrate his attention to and consideration for his patient. Our work with the doctor was helpful, but we had another way to project the image of listening, caring, and thoroughness. Counsel reflected that desired image as well.

Through questioning of the jurors in voir dire, opening statements, witness examinations, and closing arguments, we evaluated each strategy to be sure that what defense counsel did either reflected (or at least did not contradict) an image of listening, caring, and thoroughness. Counsel looked at the witnesses as they answered his questions instead of looking to the next question as they spoke, he showed compassion for a family that lost a beloved member, yet was thorough in questioning and presentation. In essence, he became the image of the doctor who was sitting at counsel table. He showed the jury who his client was through what he did and how he did it as the client's representative.

What happens when you don't account for this global truth? In an intellectual property dispute between two companies, the smaller company accused the larger of being a corporate "bully," unjustly taking the small company's ideas simply because it had the power and money to do so. The defendant larger company counsel was aggressive and was not afraid to show that aggression in the courtroom. During cross-examination of the small company's witnesses, the defense trial team was on the attack. It had valid information with which to impeach the witnesses, and the team attacked those issues using loud voices and an intimidating posture. Tactics similar to those of a bully.

As a reflection of its client, this trial team behaved in a manner congruent with the opposition's core theme. As a result, jurors believed the plaintiff's side of the story. That story was the most consistent with the defendant's counsel's image and behavior they saw in the courtroom.

While it is critical to focus on witnesses and be prepared with the content of your case, it is also important to take a big picture look at the image you want jurors to have of your client and your case as a whole. What adjectives do you want jurors to use to describe your client, and more importantly, what adjectives do you *not* want associated with your client? Then take a step back and honestly ask yourself (or someone else) which of those good and bad adjectives could be used to describe how you present yourself in the courtroom?

For counsel who represents individual plaintiffs, avoid an image that communicates a focus on money or wealth. If you show up in the courtroom in an expensive suit with a big, shiny, designer watch, you could be doing an injustice to your client. While some attorneys I have worked with believe that such accessories demonstrates success and are a way to garner respect from the jurors, it is more likely that presenting yourself with expensive attire and accessories signals to jurors, "this case is all about money." Presenting yourself as a professional without glitz can help jurors relate to you and your client much more effectively, and you will garner respect by effectively presenting your case, not through your Rolex.

You don't just want to present your case, you want to be your case.

In essence, you don't just want to *present* your case, you want to *be your case.* You are not the star of the show. Your client, your client's story, and its associated image are your focus. Remember, when it comes to telling a story in the courtroom, peripheral cues can be just as important as the content of the message. You are both a critical messenger and a reflection of your client.

Always.

Questions to Ask Yourself

- What are the key image messages I want relayed about my case and my client to the jurors?

- How is the manner in which I present myself either reflecting or contradicting those messages?

National Institute for Trial Advocacy